Change, Conflict, and Self-Determination

NEXT STEPS IN RELIGIOUS EDUCATION

BOOKS BY IRIS V. CULLY
Published by The Westminster Press

The Dynamics of Christian Education

Children in the Church

Imparting the Word:
  The Bible in Christian Education

Christian Worship and Church Education

Change, Conflict, and Self-Determination:
  Next Steps in Religious Education

In collaboration with Kendig Brubaker Cully

An Introductory Theological Wordbook

Change, Conflict, and Self-Determination

NEXT STEPS
IN RELIGIOUS EDUCATION

by

Iris V. Cully

THE WESTMINSTER PRESS
Philadelphia

Scripture quotations from the Revised Standard Version of the Bible are copyright, 1946 and 1952, by the Division of Christian Education of the National Council of Churches, and are used by permission.

BOOK DESIGN BY DOROTHY ALDEN SMITH

Published by The Westminster Press ®
Philadelphia, Pennsylvania

PRINTED IN THE UNITED STATES OF AMERICA

Library of Congress Cataloging in Publication Data

Cully, Iris V.
  Change, conflict, and self-determination.

  Includes bibliographical references.
  1. Religious education—Philosophy. I. Title.
BV1464.C85   268   72-5582
ISBN 0-664-20954-8

To
Elizabeth Fowlkes Miller
and
Randolph Crump Miller

Contents

Part III
THE MEDIUM: EDUCATION

Preface

THE religious community has always recognized that it has an educational task. It has known that the young need to be nurtured and adults confirmed in their understanding. And all members need continual reminders and renewals to keep their faith strong. There have been two aspects of this educational task. One is concerned with life within the community; the other, with witnessing the faith to outsiders.

In order to accomplish such goals both content and method are important. Christianity has been strongly oriented toward content, and this concern for correct understanding has stimulated theological thinking of a high order. It has also led to divisiveness within the church and oppression of those outside it. Thus content of the Christian faith is too momentous a factor to be disregarded. Even within that small sector known as American Protestantism during the twentieth century there have been several conflicting emphases: a fundamentalist piety, a struggle over science and religion, a liberal theological emphasis within "mainstream" Protestantism, and an accompanying hardening of orthodoxy among conservatives. The neo-orthodox ascendancy, stemming from European theology, beginning in the 1930's, has fallen apart. What predominant theological theme will emerge cannot at this time be foreseen. There are similar variations in Biblical studies.

The educator takes content as a given. The educative process is a way by which Bible, history (tradition), belief (theology), worship, and witness become incorporated into the lives of individuals and congregations. The educator looks at life (in this case the life of the church) from this stance. He is a member who is equipped to perceive educational implications in the life and activity of the church and to help in directing or redirecting such an activity. This makes the educator part of a team that has particular skills and competencies that are placed in the service of the church. It does not mean that an educational viewpoint dominates, but it could mean that the church is not endlessly canceling out its own efforts, as, for example, when one theological stance is indicated in hymns and another in preaching, when one Biblical view is used as a basis for a children's curriculum and another in an adult class. If diversity were deliberately cultivated, this would have its own value. But where diverse viewpoints have been held by groups that never faced their differences, the result has been confusion and dissension within the community.

Today education, like theology, is at a point where creative innovation is possible. First it was shaken by an insistent cry for more effective subject matter learning. Now comes the demand of the economically deprived that their children be taught effectively in order to develop potentialities. The enhancement of diversity is the challenging problem set before all educators. This has important implications for religious educators.

In 1958 I became participant in the theological-educational dialogue then in progress through the book *The Dynamics of Christian Education.* In the closing paragraph I wrote these words:

> Only dynamic methods can fully carry it [the teaching that arises from the proclamation of the gospel] so that the work of bringing light and life to men may continue. Periodically those responsible for the teaching work of the church need

to check their methods and materials against contemporary ecumenical understanding of the needs of the people for whom it was given and to whom it is addressed.

This volume is intended to carry on that task.

My husband, Kendig Brubaker Cully, has also participated in this task: in writing, teaching, and the parish. This book would not be complete without acknowledgment of his painstaking assistance in final preparation of the manuscript. More important has been the stimulus and encouragement of our shared life and love together.

I. V. C.

Springhill
Belmont, Vermont

Part I

THE SETTING: SPACESHIP EARTH

Chapter 1

Culture as Environment

THE teaching ministry of the church is at an interchange. This can be demonstrated by looking at denominational structures, course offerings at theological schools, curricular options for the parish, and voiced concerns of both clergy and laity. One always knows when an interchange is approaching, but there can still be confusion when the options come into view and the realization flashes on the mind that whatever decision is made will determine the direction for some time to come. The next exit is a long way down the road.

As religious education approaches such a point, many segments of the church have decided that continuing along the same route brings decreasing results, yet the enterprise itself is built into the responsibility of the Christian community. Which turn will be taken, and where will this lead? The church has the power to determine the direction of change, provided conflicts do not result merely in confusion and the temptation to abandon the enterprise. This is the future to be faced. It has already stimulated attempts to discern patterns and shape alternatives. The necessity is seen not only in religious education but in all the enterprises of church, nation, and culture—indeed throughout the totality of today's world.

The peoples of earth seem suddenly to have been released into visions of the future. The Third World nations have hope of longer and fuller life based on the possibility of developing dormant resources in their lands and people. The so-called developed nations find themselves confused because the nineteenth-century vision—that progress through technology would bring happiness—has turned to ashes. The "century of progress" envisioned by a world's fair, the "Christian century" hoped for by a periodical only then beginning, has not evolved in the intended way. Rather, the result seems to be a planet whose ecology is damaged, where weaponry is capable of easily destroying all living things, and where there are increasing gaps between the rich and the poor.

Seemingly mired in desperate problems, the prevailing mood turns aside from this reality into one of imagining, dreaming, and fantasizing. Thoughts are turned toward the year 2000, an almost mystical number now only one generation away. Projections of the future are in the air, and futurology has become a study if not a science. Prediction is no longer considered naïve or evasive. The assumption is made that only by deliberately looking with seriousness toward a future can one have any control over its development. Usually people have let themselves be governed by events and have made decisions on the basis of what was happening to them. Mistakenly, so it is said, the past has been the pattern for the future. If an event has happened in one way, it was supposed that in some form the same event would repeat itself. Families, business, government, religion—all were predicated on such an expectation.

Not so, say the futurologists. The coming future will be so different from the past as to have no precedent.[1] The new method is to think freely, unstructuredly. Creative thinking is to make hypotheses, "educated" guesses, project possible modes of action, test these, and modify accordingly. The dream becomes the future.

CHANGE

Yet those who are most uncomfortable in the present more frequently desire a return to some prior stable equilibrium. This is the situation of some people today.

Basic to the discomfort is the rapidity of change. The movement is not gradual so that one can get used to some change and, when comfortable, move on. Nor is it possible to accept change according to an individual's ability to assimilate. Change is not something individuals elect, but something in which whole groups are engulfed. This can be illustrated within the religious community by the turning from an institution-serving concern to one of involvement in the social scene. Specifically it has meant reallocation of budgets, a shifting of staffs with resultant unemployment, new forms of ministry, and new types of clergy. The result has sometimes been a drastic cut in administrative income as the laity voted with their pocketbooks; there has been a repudiation of national staffs as known faces left and new portfolios appeared, and open friction between clergy and people.

Change did not remain at this level. It reached into most of the events and attitudes that had held religious meaning for laity and many clergy. The service of worship was changed, the version of Scripture read was changed, the language of prayer was changed. The Sunday certainties were gone. Nor were there any promises that the new forms were more than trial (or, more ominously, "experimental") liturgies. The paperback revolution had reached the sanctuary, and dog-eared service books replaced the formal and familiar leather or cloth-bound volumes. People expecting solace in the existential trials of life found that their clergymen were impatient with such mundane needs. For purposes of reeducation, sermons became socially oriented. The church was busy with witnessing in the community; there was less time for the strengthening of personal relationships, a keynote of ministry twenty years earlier.

The valued layman was not the one who had led the canvass or masterminded the annual fair, but the one who was in the thick of political reform and school redirection.

People are religious for many reasons. One is that religion enables them to maintain equilibrium despite the buffetings of life, through the experience of corporate worship, the reassurance clergy can give in times of stress, and the reinforcement of their personal beliefs and devotional life. How can an essentially conservative people be helped to acquiesce in change—even if they may never eagerly reach out toward it?

Alvin Toffler's book *Future Shock* is addressed to this question. He sees the dilemma in which people are caught as they face a swiftly approaching future while needing desperately to pause. They are, he says, in a state of shock. When this is realized, one can then ask what steps to take in order to aid recovery. Are there ways of insulating people so that they can respond to change in slow stages?

> It is the thesis of this book that there are discoverable limits to the amount of change that the human organism can absorb, and that by endlessly accelerating change without first determining these limits, we may submit masses of men to demands they simply cannot tolerate.[2]

Each year brings its provocative vision, and although the popularity of a book wanes, the thought engendered remains. "Protean man" was Robert Lifton's prototype of the new generation.[3] No longer is the model "Apollonian man," the thinker, or even that primordial man of action, Prometheus, but the mythical creature who continually changed shape as necessity dictated. Charles Reich briefly popularized the phrase "Consciousness III,"[4] meaning that new kind of awareness in youth that looks confidently toward the future without having any need to build upon the past.

Such a view of humankind conflicts with the belief that each generation is founded in the being and work of its predecessors. Where change is defined as modification, it is acceptable to "revive" the past—for example, by returning to early types of liturgies, strange as the forms may seem at first; but it is disturbing to seek new forms of worship whose link with the tradition is tenuous. Good works have always been part of Christian witness, but enabling the poor to achieve equality on their own is not in the Gospels and therefore is suspect to some believers. Clergy have customarily exercised political strategy in the church but have not been expected to do so in the community.

POWER

Another element in the culture that disturbs religious people is the current emphasis on power. To be sure, power has always been an elemental factor in human relationships, but previously it had been dealt with secretly, even deviously. One did not talk about it or describe its development, although the manifestations were clear and abundant. It is disturbing to have that which is hidden revealed, especially something that in an unveiled form may be frightening or ugly. Power considered in its root meaning of "dynamic" is simply the force through which any action is accomplished and may be beneficent or demonic. Only by analyzing the sources, types, and expressions of power can one make a judgment. Analysis of power structures in church and community becomes an important way of discovering the effects, if any, of the Christian meanings of existence. No longer need people be resigned to accepting incompetence or injustice. No longer need people live under the illusion that ameliorative efforts will have enduring effect. When people become sensitized to the specific realities of power, they almost have to realize that each person, no matter how withdrawn or seemingly inoffensive, is involved in the power structure (if only because by inaction one has voted particular power structures into being). This is an uncomfortable thought to people who have believed that one could be indifferent to and withdrawn from the arena of power politics. No one likes to be stripped of illusions, and those who rest comfortably in "doing good" or "avoiding trouble" do not like to learn that what they thought was for good could be turned to evil uses. For example, it is "shocking" to find that not all the materials designated for the relief of the poor are used for that purpose.

The study of power finds its technical form in game theory, which plots the strategies by which aims are accomplished within social and political situations. The term "war games" has had long usage, and game theory reaches into many areas of life.[5] In the most sophisticated form it becomes systems analysis, studies of which come under headings of mathematics, economics, finance, business, politics, sociology, psychology, and education. The overlap of systems analysis with game theory occurs because of the formal connection of each study with "rules," logical steps to be taken, and results that can be essayed but not predicted. Essentially, systems analysis is a way of effecting change or solving problems by setting forth options, researching the possibilities for success, developing criteria for evaluation, choosing one or more areas for development, gathering resources for implementation, making evaluations, and from the results (feedback) modifying the plan or eliminating it in favor of another option. This is a continuing "game," which is forever modifiable through the constant interaction of input (evaluation) with the restructuring of output (design in action).

This must be taken seriously because in recent years almost every large ecclesiastical structure has been restructured with the intention of making the administration functional. Committees have become "task forces" in expectation that these will perform a task and then disband. This may not be realistic, for tasks have a tendency to continue, to fill up the terms of the members on the force. Decentralization has dispersed field people to live in the areas that they are supposedly fielding. For example, in this kind of reshuffling, within some ecclesiastical administrations, religious education has become subsumed under parish, teaching ministry, or simply ministry, with the result that the professional staff is dispersed. Within the Catholic structures, catechetics has been lifted into new prominence with area training centers to prepare lay teachers and graduate study centers to professionalize diocesan and parish coordinators.[6]

This is one result of the application of systems analysis within an organizational setup. Such an attempt to look at organizations and perceive their functions in different ways inevitably suggests threatening change. The negative effects in human terms—lost jobs or unaccustomed work—becomes a problem, and resistance runs high. The inhumane possibilities of technology applied to human situations become overt. Are people indeed figures to be moved around the board: go forward two steps, go back five steps, move off the board? The theological implications of change and of the use of power need exploration, for the situation described is common in American life.

In the consideration of power, human factors seem to move with reference to an overarching organizational purpose.[7] It is possible to use current forms for sensitivity training to facilitate change. Forms of personal therapy within group therapy, epitomized by awareness and encounter sessions, have become popular.[8] It is as if people caught in difficult social and economic situations hoped for relief through some form of personal or marital renewal. One church official can say "We are seeking a Christian way to dismiss x number of employees because our priorities have moved in other directions and their jobs are no longer needed." The ethical dilemma posed by this statement is not sensed.

Concern about the use of power is indicated by current studies of aggression that seek to discover whether the human being is naturally aggressive and needs to have such drives curbed and redirected in order that the species may survive.[9] Is humankind naturally trusting and interdependent until distorted into destructive aggression by culture and conditioning? It would seem to some that the present pattern of aggressiveness, far from ensuring survival, is leading to destruction.

A society that values aggressiveness and rewards the show of power by the marks of success, has little place for the weak. The sick are not treated with compassion because they are sick, but only if they can pay for treatment. The old are not honored for their years, but only if they have been able to save enough money to appear young or to stay decently hidden when senile. The young are well treated and rewarded only as long as they can contain themselves in disciplined fashion. The poor are denounced as evil or incompetent. Yet there have been times and places in which the poor are considered under the special concern of God—and heaven knows they need it. Those in institutions for any reason are shut away at the level of bare existence with little meaningful activity and no future. Those with power have overcome the powerless. Yet only the truly strong can be tender, loving, and compassionate. Power can be used beneficently and distributed in such a way that the weak are enabled to help themselves. The really strong do not need the "weak" to serve their needs.

SELF-DETERMINATION

Self-determination is another factor in the cultural environment that poses the threat of change to those who have kept secure by arranging life for others. Hence it arouses conflict and brings out the strategies of power. On the international scene, the power of Western peoples to govern those in Asia, Africa, and the ocean islands has been broken. The task of becoming a nation is a slow and painful one that involves uncovering the past, developing workable political and social structures, and envisioning a creative future. What began as a revolt from the political dominance of Western nations has become a determination to overcome economic dominance.

This liberation to self-determination pertains to a whole group but not necessarily to individuals within the group. Among most of the peoples of the world the individual finds identity as a member of a closely knit group. Liberation does not mean personal freedom in the accepted Western sense. Liberation is new life for tribe or nation. The individual is expected to acquiesce in group action.

One voice of the newly liberated is Frantz Fanon, who was born in Martinique, worked in Algeria, studied medicine in France, practiced in the Antilles, and died in the United States at the age of thirty-six. His book *The Wretched of the Earth* struck a note far beyond the specific struggle to which he addressed himself. It has now become a strategic educational document.[10]

Self-determination in the United States and Canada means eliminating the illusion of the "melting pot." Each immigrant supposedly shed his heritage and became engrafted to the American past. French settlers, in Canada from its beginnings, were powerless because they were a conquered minority. Blacks, in the United States before the landing of the *Mayflower*, were long considered nonpersons. The original people of the land, misnamed Indians, were sequestered in reservations through systematic acts that to later Indians appeared to be intended genocide. Only today is their own history being recorded.[11] Spanish-speaking Americans assert the right to use their native language. A Protestant-oriented view ignores the fact that Spanish Catholic culture predated English culture in Florida and in California. Jews are renewing their cultural ties with one another around the world and finding new meanings in the symbols of their people. Ethnic groups are recovering their European roots. Even white Anglo-Saxon Protestants are beginning to explore their own distinctiveness while uneasily trying to discover how they can be one member-group of a plural society.

When peoples assert themselves, the resultant necessity for the dominant group to restructure its self-perception is a painful process. Some avoid the task and act as if the prior *status quo* were still in existence. Others become hostile and vent destructive anger on their newly assertive compatriots.

THE TEACHING MINISTRY AND CONFLICT

These, then, are the conditions of our culture: (*a*) a time of rapid change, which many people find difficult to face; (*b*) a situation in which power is being analyzed and people are being forced to admit that everyone has a part in the power structure, even when passive; (*c*) a world in which self-determination is the order of the day (symbolized by the ever-growing number of flags at United Nations Plaza) and where self-awareness brings new assertions of identity to minority groups within a nation. These factors spell conflict, which is the key word binding the whole together.

What is the teaching ministry of the religious community in an environment of conflict? The Christian gospel is filled with phrases such as "Blessed are the peacemakers," "Love your enemies," "Turn the other cheek," "Forgive to seventy times seven," "Put up your sword," "Do not be angry." The impulse of the religious person has been to ignore or deny that conflict exists and to repress the signs. This is useless. Only a situation brought into the open can be dealt with in a positive way. Equally fruitless is the habit religious people have sometimes had of moralizing and verbalizing. The gospel does not do this. The words of the gospel are both descriptions and prescriptions of how the person who lives by God's grace can act in situations of conflict.[12]

The gospel is practical: "If you are offering your gift at the altar and there remember that your brother has something against you, leave your gift there before the altar and go; first be reconciled to your brother and then come and offer your gift" (Matt. 5:23, 24). There is the wisdom of Paul: "Be angry but do not sin; do not let the sun go down on your anger" (Eph. 4:26). The teaching ministry should sensitize people to the elements in conflict situations, enabling people to become participants in reconciliation. The processes interact and could be individual or group encounters.

Conflict leads people into negative action when they feel weak and fearful. Those who have learned to trust God need not be fearful.[13] Whatever happens within the community to develop strength and trust is a positive factor in helping people deal with conflict. The congregation should be the kind of supportive community that does this for its members. No parish can bring Christian witness into the conflicts of community and world if individual lives are fearful and their collective identity within the church is weak. As long as people need a great deal of personal support, they will be unable to be supportive of wider efforts. At the same time, if they are required to give support to one another, in that action each can become stronger and have the possibility of growing beyond attention to personal needs.

Change engenders conflict. They interact. Learning how to confront change and to use conflict positively is a teaching task. Conflict arises whenever a person feels it is necessary to accommodate words, opinions, style, attitudes, or actions to the needs of another or of a group, as in committee discussion, family argument, community tension, or war between nations. But learning to understand the dynamics of conflict has its own methodology. This involves developing mutual trust within the group, which allows people to look at the factors without threat, in the assurance that no one will be destroyed because someone else is given strength. Power does not need to be traded; there is enough and to spare for all uses. Until the year 2000 and beyond, the governing boards of congregations will face conflict with the options of resolving it through force (the strongest, loudest, most prestigious wins), through compromise (acquiescence without satisfaction), through consensus (which may be an illusion), or through slowly working out a creative solution that seeks to fuse new elements into the situation.

Every organization in a church faces conflict. Every class situation becomes involved in conflict. The teachers of children call this "discipline problems"; with adolescents it takes various forms of restiveness; with adults it will sometimes be seen as passivity. To withdraw from conflict is sometimes seen as being courteous and even as exercising a religious act of forbearance.

When the people of a parish have consciously learned how to handle conflict in this limited and fairly safe group, they might be induced to consider the subject of conflict within the larger community, and their role in dealing with it constructively. Whether they choose to act as a congregation or as individuals is less important than that they see the necessity of positive involvement.

Everyone finds potential situations of conflict within family life, arising frequently from the dynamics of change, power, and self-determination. Tools for dealing with interpersonal conflict can be worked out through situations where people give mutual support as they learn, or through individual or family counseling, which is in its own way a learning situation.

The conflict that arises from the self-determination of minorities has been one of the most difficult situations facing the Christian church in many years, often threatening to dissolve congregations and split denominations. This form of conflict cannot be met by a purely intellectual process. Verbalizing about the brotherhood of man under God is no substitute for giving all people access to jobs, housing, and education. Paulo Freire[14] reminds his readers that reform is not the same as revolution, for reform changes only a few factors in order to encourage acceptance of the *status quo* by easing the disabilities of the poor. Revolution is a complete changing around, a restructuring of one's perception of the self as fully human, acting in one's own behalf. Freire would bring about this kind of revolution through an education in which people look at the problems that keep them in poverty, act to achieve equality in the political and economic scene, and reflect at each step on what is happening. But he does not address the question of how to educate those in power to accept such change.

Hence there arises the necessity for an education to help the satisfied to cope with change they neither seek nor desire. The

familiar and the habitual are comfortable. Maintaining established socioeconomic barriers is useful. One of the conflict-
laden passages of Scripture is Mary's song: "He has put down
the mighty from their thrones, and exalted those of low degree; he has filled the hungry with good things, and the rich
he has sent empty away" (Luke 1:52–53). No compromise
here! Not everyone is given power; not everyone is filled. The
roles are reversed, as are those of Lazarus and Dives in the
parable told by Jesus (Luke 16:19–31). This is uncomfortable
material for many of the devout. The dispossessed are not willing to see it as a paradigm of eternal life. Nor can it be ex-
plained in the light of the national aspirations of Israel or the
Messianic expectations of the Jews. People have always interpreted Scripture as the word of God to them and to their
day. Mary's song becomes a word of judgment today.

The prophets of Israel have insights for people in the midst
of change. Amos shouted that the poor had been sold for a pair
of shoes (Amos 2:6), and he scorned those who lived in ivory
houses (Amos 3:15). This is not a didactic passage, but the
words are meant as condemnation and warning of the judgment of God. People who are made uncomfortable by changes
in the words and the order of liturgy are hardly prepared for
Amos' assertion that the whole worship of the people of God
has become hateful to the Lord because of their unrighteous-
ness (Amos 5:21–23). To what then can the insecure cling?

Education for conflict and for change must presuppose a
commitment in the community of the church through which
members can serve God with joy and support one another in
mutual confidence.[15] This is the learning and living environment through which Christians are nurtured. Then, by searching the Scriptures, by the mutual strengthening of the liturgy,
through an understanding of what it means to live as a Christian, through action in real situations where justice cries aloud,
by thoughtful consideration of what has been accomplished
and what needs strengthening, a continuing situation of education for change can develop.

"Change is the great constant with which we live," affirmed

an editorial writer, noting the reassuring passage of the seasons.[16] The Bible affirms for believers the reliability of God through all the changes in the world. He works through the power of his Holy Spirit. He calls each person by a name. These are the religious realities to be set alongside the concepts governing contemporary life.

CONCLUSIONS

People can be helped to face change and the ensuing conflict (1) when they can admit the existence of conflict; (2) when they have feelings of personal security to enable them to admit the claims of others; (3) when they can internalize as an attitude what they have previously defined intellectually as an ethical course; (4) when they can indicate acceptance of change by responding positively to it, joining willingly in a new situation.

The processes by which this is accomplished are: (1) developing within the congregation an environment of security that is positive, accepting, and mutually strengthening; (2) deepening a personal faith and trust in God; (3) acting in new ways within a situation as individuals singly and within groups; (4) reflecting and evaluating actions in the light of common Christian understandings; (5) testing new attitudes in the facing of situations of increasing threat, combined with increased reassurance when possible.

Chapter 2

People Live Here

PERSONS are the focus of ministry. With all they hold in common, they also have highly individualized characteristics. There appear to be unique needs for special age groups, sometimes standing out so sharply as to be a source of intergenerational conflict and causing disruptions within the community. Yet there is always an interdependence among the generations. A suburban enclave consisting primarily of young couples and their elementary-school-age children has its own form of ingrownness. Communities for the elderly provide a welcome buffer from the exuberance of the young, which can in time become tedious. Adolescents, as much as they enjoy each other's company, are usually attached to the rest of the community. Actually, the church is the only agency that involves persons of every age and dignifies each stage of life from birth through death.

YOUTH

All over the world, the segment of humanity arousing the most concern is youth. No longer is "youth" to be identified with adolescence, the years between twelve and eighteen or twenty-one. The psychologist Kenneth Keniston has affirmed that there is a life stage beyond adolescence which he calls "youth." This is his conclusion after observing young people at a time of alienation, radical commitment, and dissent.[1] During this period (not earlier as Erik Erikson has stated)[2] youth explore life-styles, investigate areas of study, try out modes of work, and become aware of each other sexually. Not until the late twenties will they develop a real sense of direction sufficient for them to choose a field of work and a marriage partner.

Moreover, many youth, including adolescents, have evolved elements for a life-style that seems strange to the generations beyond them. Theodore Roszak terms this a "counter-culture."

> The interests of our college-age and adolescent young in the psychology of alienation, oriental mysticism, psychedelic drugs, and communitarian experiments comprise a cultural constellation that radically diverges from values and assumptions that have been in the mainstream of our society at least since the Scientific Revolution of the seventeenth century. But I am aware that this constellation has much maturing to do before its priorities fall into place and before any well-developed social cohesion grows up around it.[3]

He goes on to describe their alternative as "dressed in a garish motley, its costume borrowed from many and exotic sources— from depth psychiatry, from the mellowed remnants of left-wing ideology, from the oriental religions, from Romantic Weltschmerz, from anarchistic social theory, from Dada and American Indian lore, and, I suppose, the perennial wisdom." [4] For him, this is a justified revolt against a society characterized by the denaturing of man through technological involvements.

Margaret Mead, who has studied "coming of age" since her early book on Samoa in 1928,[5] sees a complete transformation in the cultural role of youth. Formerly, the young learned their life patterns from the old; recently the young have been taking patterns from the peer group. Now the whole process is reversed: the older generation must learn from the young.[6] Considering what was said in the previous chapter about the resistance to change among adults, this suggests a high degree of conflict.

The life-style among this experimental segment of the young is an affirmation that life is good and is to be enjoyed. Neither work nor achievement is the aim. These young people reject the goals for which they have seen middle-class society striving. They have seen success turn to ashes; they have seen alcoholism in the family, divorce related to work pressures, constant uprooting of the family, the promotion that never came, the premature heart attack. The work ethic has seemed destructive. Those born wealthy have options for creativity. The poor have never had enough security for real living, and working hard has not brought them "success." Voluntary poverty is a subtle way of life, seldom worked out since the first generation of the Franciscans. It survives perhaps among some orders of Buddhist monastics today. Some Protestant religious communities struggle for adequate living on the economic terms of American society: they set up a factory or farm and let everyone work. Integrity of work, rather than enjoyment through minimal work, is a goal.

But the cry of the young is "Get off the treadmill." Work must be creative. Significantly, one college which has had a distinctive program in engineering ceramics finds students uninterested in that approach but eager to learn ceramics as an art and a craft.

The sustaining force of life is love. Disregarding traditional barriers, youth are insisting that one can care about more than one person: they point out that serial marriage is a custom among some of the older generation (reminiscent of the long tradition of polygamy). They further affirm that security rests in sharing life within an extended family (and "family" does not necessarily mean biological relatives). Human beings should be able to live in proximity and get along in harmony, mutual understanding, support, and helpfulness, they say. This basic premise would hardly surprise minority-group families who have found that having the generations help each other was necessary for survival. It is a strange idea only to the Western nuclear family. The sexual aspects of the living arrangements of the young are of concern to society, which has always regulated sexual practice in some way. At present the old ground rules are ignored and no new ones have been fully accepted. This uncertainty concerns not only premarital sex but extramarital relations, the permissible extent of divorce and remarriage, and the living arrangements of the elderly.

The dress of a person or group is an expression of the self-image. Museum exhibits suggest that quick alterations in fashion have been the norm in the Western world for some generations, although modifications of style are more apparent to the observer from year to year than they are to one studying costume historically. The distinctive factor today is that the young are choosing their own styles, looking for one that will not be copied by their elders.

Youth's conflict with the dominating adult world has been alternatively violent and passive. While family tension had been an accepted part of growing up, active revolt in the school (rather than passive resistance) was a new phenomenon. Peers imitate each other and the revolt that began in the university ended in junior high schools. Sometimes it began in racial tensions, backed by parental attitudes; sometimes the revolt voiced the anger the young felt at being required to accept a logic for education that made no sense to them.

Alternatively, some young people chose passivity. The use of drugs reached epidemic proportions, peaked, and may have begun to decline. Epidemics of physical disease are carefully noted, but epidemics of other kinds have not been recognized in the same way. The treatment of physiological disease could be a model for looking at psychological disease.[7] Suicide and the high incidence of automobile accidents among the young are other examples. Passivity may be indicated also by the willingness to drop out of school, the desire to prolong schooling, and an unwillingness to make a commitment to work or marriage until the late twenties. These might be forecasts of a new life-style in which the traditional adult tasks are assumed at a later age, which makes sense in relation to longevity and early retirement.

Rock music and involvement in multimedia experiences are characteristic of youth, who tend to become totally enveloped in whatever they do. Cinema, too, has become total experience through new forms of plot and new styles of camera work. (Film-making is one of their skills.) Religion is part of the life of youth, although not necessarily in its traditional form. Drugs are sometimes used in the hope of experiencing transcendence. They practice forms of Hindu or Buddhist meditation so that in the silence they may know the self more intensely and relate to the transcendent more completely. The occult has drawn its followers, as we see in the widespread interest in astrology, Tarot cards, and the *I Ching*.

Furthermore, there is a new awareness of Jesus. Young people respond to him as one who loved, who had compassion, and who brought down the wrath of the establishment on his head. Their music describes this, including the currently popular *Jesus Christ Superstar*. Groups meet for worship and mutual support in whatever churches will open their doors to them. They affirm that Jesus heals them and shows them a new way of life. There is some similarity to the Pentecostal groups that are multiplying around the world, so disturbing to the established churches, who see resemblances to early Christian practice but do not feel comfortable with groups that are not orthodox in belief, worship, or life-style.

Is this generation lost to the church? Youth welcome change, are frustrated by their inability to grasp and use power, and are affirming self-determination. Hence they generate conflict. Simply bringing the guitar into church will not attract the youth, but it might distract the old. The one thing that is asked of the church it seems unable to do—namely, to accept people as they are. This means helping the basic constituency of the church to accept change and to share power. There are many acceptable forms and times of worship. Getting a maximum number of people together at the same time is of no basic importance. The fellowship of Christians cannot be interpreted so narrowly. Orthodoxy is gone; heterodoxy is the reality, even if it is not officially acknowledged. Variations in belief and practice are asked by the young because they will not stifle their doubts.

In addition to the conventional interests of congregations, there will be some developed by the young people. These may not be permanent. Colleges also have found that special projects are sometimes dropped after an initial enthusiasm.

Those who have left the church will return in their own time. The adult church can try seriously to open avenues through which young people can find expression for their needs and concerns as full members.

THE AGED

Since, as has often been remarked, youth may have more in common with their grandparents than with their parents, it is well to turn next to this group. People who have been taught that life is work and that achievement means having money are finding after a lifetime of work that they have no activity and little money. A vacuum comes into the life of the retired worker and some do not survive the trauma. The wife of a retiree continues her housework. He himself feels useless. When both have worked outside and both have assumed housekeeping roles, then in retirement each has some tasks. As equal opportunities are opened to women and minority groups, the job market shrinks and people are retired sooner. This could lead to a shorter work week for all. It could mean retirement at fifty-five, already a fact in parts of Europe.

Living on the economic margin is serious. To people who have been used to comfortable incomes, the revelation of how little a retirement income will buy comes as a shock. Belief in the efficacy of faithful work has proved false, and the response varies from cynicism and despair to rationalization. One reason why older adults drop out, from church as well as other activities, is that they have been taught they should pay their way, and so they have no awareness of the church as a community of mutual concern. Experience with the church convinced them that, theology notwithstanding, it was important to be among the pledgers.

The economics of age has another aspect with which the church has not yet dealt. Social Security pays for a married woman only as wife; if her husband dies, the widow is left with less pension. Upon remarriage she loses even that. One of the most poignant expressions of this situation was conveyed in a letter written by a widow to a newspaper columnist. She and the man she loved were living together without the legality of marriage because they could not afford to do otherwise. Now she could rent her house and keep her Social Security income. The result: neighbors were outraged, and their children disowned them. With the elderly, as with the young, a change in marriage patterns is threatening to a society. Open divorce or hidden affairs are condoned. The openly illegal is considered immoral. The church will gladly comfort the widowed as long as they live alone. The new situation is awkward.

Power was a theme in the previous chapter, and the loss of power is one of the deepest sources of helplessness on the part of the elderly—the loss of power both as physical health and as influence. Since only power brings respect in this society, the old are not even respected. Aside from a few elderly leaders of the world or nation, the influence of the old is negligible.

But the most formidable problem of the old in Western society is how to die with dignity. Here, too, an ethical problem is avoided by those most involved: the professionals in medicine, law, and religion. The dread of lying helplessly for months and even years at a great expense that will impoverish the living, is a part of every older person's life. The church, which could take a creative, affirmative part in this question, simply sends the minister to visit. When is death natural and when is it euthanasia? The question is serious. Cultures that practice abortion and infanticide have frequently also practiced "senilicide."

Perhaps the basic need of older people can be found in Erikson's delineation of life stages.[8] His third stage of adulthood is "integrity vs. despair and disgust." In these later years, it is imperative to be able to affirm the rightness of one's own life-style and to recognize death as part of the life cycle. Alternatively one becomes cynical and fearful of approaching death. This continues a process of separation begun earlier with the disengagement from children, from work, and from power. Finally it means accepting the death of the mate and the self. This task is made more difficult in a culture that ignores death, masks it, and has a cult of youth. Sometimes the religious ceremonies of death may offer little to help with the task symbolically, partly because even Christians may have only a halfhearted hope in eternal life. There are few Stoics, and it is only now beginning to be admitted that everyone fears death. Psychologists are becoming involved with doctors in helping the dying and their families to accept this final fact of life.[9] Death is the final form of change, as the apostle Paul affirmed in writing to a congregation about death and resurrection (I Cor. 15:51–53). In the resurrection, the Scriptures say, Christ has overcome the *power* of death.

Rituals are a necessary way of actualizing the unfathomable dimensions of life. The synagogue continues the weekly memorial service through which families commemorate their dead. The Catholic Christian tradition has possibilities of memorial and celebration within All Souls' Day and All Saints' Day. It is possible that in the emphasis on the good news of the resurrection, reiterated each Sunday, the church ignores (except once a year) the fact that death always precedes resurrection. Mutual strengthening through faith comes as the religious community interprets the tradition in worship, in study, through the pastoral office, and in the mutual ministry of one person to another.

The elderly pose to the church problems analogous to those

of youth: if money is valued, they do not have it; if activities are important, those of the church are irrelevant; they may not conform to the accepted life-style. They raise important ethical questions of life, love, and death that no one seems willing to grapple with seriously. To educate for the acceptance of death as the completion of life, to educate for life as quietude, we have no tools, no methods, and few materials.[10]

BEING THE MIDDLE GENERATION:
IS IT WORTH THE STRUGGLE?

The work of the world and of the church is done primarily by people in the working years between twenty-five and sixty. This is known as "the prime of life." The expression epitomizes the fullness of physical and mental power and all the subtle uses of power that society assigns within the life of work, family, and community. It is also a time for playing a role, assuming obligations, even putting on a front. Psychological adjustment devices are aimed at helping this age group to deal with their problems—from sensitivity training, to improving relationships within the working groups, to marathons, to helping them let down their defenses and face their needs. Marriage counseling deals not only with the subtle problems of relationships but even teaches couples how to have intercourse. Into what strange necessities has culture led, when the obvious becomes difficult! It is as if living together were almost impossible.

Marriage and work are the poles of adult existence. Work preempts most of life and for those in higher income brackets it frequently includes lengthy business trips and many changes of residence. The aggressiveness required in a competitive situation can be exhausting. The poor may strive long hours without success and frequently withdraw. Alcoholism is a form of withdrawal practiced rather widely in this age group across socioeconomic lines. In the twenties and thirties responsibility for children is heavy and can become overwhelming, financially and emotionally. A study of marriage disclosed that there was more stability among childless couples and among those whose children had left home than among those for whom conflict over decisions concerning children added a strain to the relationship.

Marriage as the other basic involvement of middle adulthood may or may not be a strengthening relationship. It can make work bearable and life satisfying. It can also be a testing ground for one's vocational uncertainties and the frustrations people feel in the disuse of their abilities. Experiments in sexual relations are not confined to the young or to the old. The middle group have both traditional extramarital outlets and currently the new group experiments. But the middle generation find themselves to be the arbiters of morality for society, and so are caught in a dilemma wherein they must affirm one code even though practicing another.[11]

The church may ignore these factors, treat them on a superficial level, or overlay them with activities. Sometimes active participation in church events can be a person's way of doing penance or of covering up pain with activity. Where this serves immediate needs, it is useful. If no effort is made to recognize and bring healing to deeper needs, activity becomes an evasion. The church has an educational ministry here, recognized or not. The work that goes on in the church reflects the work in other parts of the community. Here the premises, ethics, and real functions of the activities need to be tested with reference to Christian meanings. Such reflection forms part of the lifestyle of the Christian community. Actions become internalized as beliefs. The decision-making actions of a church are important in the religious education of its adults. The "tone" of a parish is important. It could be suffused with joy, or it could merely talk about joy while being heavily laden with bills to pay, activities to complete, and the routine of Sunday worship. A joyful community makes a positive context from which Christian families can reflect on their life together and on their work. Life in the church could be a "model" for life in other community agencies. Whether or not the church should be involved in community change, let it be remembered that each member of a parish is personally involved in the life of that community. The church equips these people.

The middle generation people have power: in family, church, and community. They struggle with their own self-determination while being concurrently involved in the demands made upon them by others. They tend to acquiesce in change—or perhaps they are unaware of it when it moves at a rate comfortable to them. They are involved in many kinds of conflict. Some of them wonder whether achievement has been worth the struggle because of the effects it has had on family and on the sense of personal well-being.

WOMEN FEEL THEY ARE A SPECIAL CASE

In a time of change, when everyone is conscious of where power lies, a revolt among fifty percent of the population is not to be taken lightly. Some form of liberation came to women through religious reformers who mitigated the legal rigors of marriage through religious restraints. Jesus affirmed that men could not divorce arbitrarily; Mohammed permitted his followers four wives only. Political and legal liberation came gradually during the nineteenth century, culminating in the right to vote. The present women's movement has erupted in several directions, making women aware of continuing inequalities. Primarily this involves a change of perception on the part of all people, which is why it is intrinsically revolutionary. Women are no longer willing to be described in men's terms or to be measured in men's categories by men's standards. They want human categories to encompass the varieties of abilities and experiences of men and women, permitting women to be aggressive and men to be gentle. Stereotypes are rejected. There has arisen a generation of fathers who feel comfortable taking care of children and sharing household tasks. The crux of the matter comes in the insistence of women that they shall be able to use their abilities fully in specific vocations. It means equal opportunity to rise to positions of power in work and in political life.[12]

Marriage brings fulfillment, for man and for woman, when each gives the other the opportunity to grow into fullness of life. With an emphasis on "population zero," some women will decide not to have children. Bearing children does not bring a sense of fulfillment to all. When the pressure to reproduce is removed, only those who desire parenthood will raise families. More women, married or unmarried, will have careers as their basic life pattern.

The happiest outcome of the women's liberation movement would be the liberation of humankind. Men need liberation to choose more freely their lifework, to continue in it with less pressure and to develop real leisure activities. This could bring them longer life and fewer pressure-caused disabilities. It could also redirect aggressive drives to positive ends, bringing a diminution of strife, a less eager pursuit of goods and power, and a more serene existence for humankind.

The church did not begin the women's liberation movement. Segments of the church still refuse women ordination. Others enforce celibacy in specialized situations. Women have little influence in the power structure. The response of a bureaucracy under pressure is to elect a member of the protesting group to a term as president, while the real power lies with the continuously reelected executives. In parish practice, women raise auxiliary funds with typical women's activities. This is satisfying for those who wish to participate, but these activities could equally well use male help. Women rarely give a monetary value to their work. Their time is seldom subtracted as an expense from the total income of an activity. This image of women is transferred through church periodicals, curricular materials, and reports. It is reinforced by the approval given when women stay within stereotyped roles and by the opposition exerted when they attempt to change the system. Girls have few models of women to follow in significant church roles.

Since the restructuring of perception is considered an educational task, it should be an educational priority for the church. When women function in unaccustomed roles, other participants become accustomed to accepting the fact. People then justify to themselves their new perception by intellectual means and eventually even their attitude changes. What must be accepted can usually be encompassed by all except the most rigid personalities, who will always need special help, short of being permitted to block justice and righteousness.

And Then . . .

There can not be a chapter about people that does not include children. Religious education has always meant children; this has been the case to such an extent that what happens to adults educationally has been only of peripheral concern. Yet children are taught by adults—by their parents, their teachers, and their fellow church members.

Actions and attitudes are reflected by the adults who are with children and in the materials and methods used. Children are sensitive to marriage, work, and community. They are aware of minority groups and their situations. They have older relatives and neighbors. Adolescents are their favorite "sitters." The whole world impinges on the child through television. Children's ears pick up whatever the adults say, and make their own sense of the world as they experience it. Change is so rapid at their age as to be almost part of their being. It strikes with force when they move to a new community or when divorce brings a new parent. The church can become a helping community aware of such needs.

More use could be made of whole family and of whole parish learning situations.[13] Particular kinds of learning can take place in such a setting, where old and young teach each other. Parents learn their role in religious education as they watch and listen to children. Teachers and parents share with one another.

Children are aware of power, being themselves a powerless

minority. The most difficult task of education is that of helping a person grow into autonomy, avoiding both the discipline that leads to passivity and the lack of discipline that prevents full development. Children reflect in their relationships with others the way in which power is used with them. Children can be tyrants in the family and in the neighborhood. Older children can be bullies. Recall the cartoon of the man who was reprimanded by the boss, who then spoke sharply to his wife, who then got angry with the child, who kicked the dog, who dashed for the cat, who put up his back.

THE END IS THE BEGINNING

The church's educational process revolves around the pace of change, the forms of power, the drive toward self-determination, and the possibilities for conflict within that kind of constellation.

The methods that the church uses in educating people will be shaped by several factors:

1. How the church faces change within its own life, locally, nationally, and around the world—including its ability to cope with social issues in terms of Christian ethics and its ability to act responsibly in an ecumenical situation.

2. How the church uses power within its own households, distributing it, understanding why people need it, monitoring its expressions so that it becomes a positive force.

3. How the church expresses the Christian faith through its liturgy, lifting Biblical words into forms and language that have meaning for its people. This involves the admission of diversity in forms and heterodoxy in meaning.

4. How the church meets the needs of people according to their generation, helping them to meet social problems, existential threats, and ethical decisions.

5. How the church helps people to act in the new situations (even revolutionary) of the time, encouraging those who dare, strengthening those who withdraw, trying to prevent violence

either from the believers in change or from those who fear the collapse of their world.

6. How the church helps people individually and in groups to reflect on personal issues in the light of their Christian faith. These have only been touched on, but they include work, sexual relations, living, dying, style of life, material and natural resources for living, and intergenerational responsibility. They involve the meaning of Christ for persons—for the young, who identify him with the rebel; for the old, who need the hope of eternal life he brings; and for all in between.

This is where people are. This is the educational task.

Chapter 3

Science: Toward Utopia or Doom?

HUMAN beings are curious. A scientific outlook can be traced back thousands of years, and is to be found not only in the scientific and mathematical principles stated by the ancient Greeks, but in astronomical observations made in places as widely separated as Mexico, England, Egypt, and China. A flowering of the scientific spirit during the European Renaissance brought a fresh wave of discovery, represented by Galileo and later Newton, and eventually Darwin and Einstein. Each scientific affirmation about the world brought its accompanying philosophy.

Western religion contributed to the rise of the modern scientific outlook.[1] The Biblical view of creation assumed order in a universe created and preserved by God. The belief in the contingency of the world upon God's action implies that one can learn about the world through observation—suggesting the inductive method. The Bible affirms the goodness of the world as the place of God's action. The scientist's exploration of the world should be congenial to the religious person and to the religious community.

SCIENCE AS AUTHORITY

The overall attitude in the modern world is to look upon empirical methods as the norm for seeking or discovering truth as well as fact. There are many aspects to this. Since an underlying world view is implicit in this attitude, these aspects should be stated.

The scientific method begins with an interaction of experiment and theory. To the practicing scientist, the two components can never fully be separated. The hypothesis has been called an act of free creative thinking. It is congenial to a person who is not bound by the confines of the already known. Experiment—that is, observations and data—grows from the hypothesis, but in turn the hypothesis is revised and reconstructed on the basis of accumulating data. Interpretation grows out of such work—the formulation of concepts, theories, and laws. The scientist realizes that there is no such thing as "pure" fact: all facts are interpretive. So the "objective" statement is one that takes into account the bias of the one who states it.

Scientific work can be tested either inductively (from the particular to the universal) or deductively (from the general to the particular), but the creative imagination of the scientist cannot be so clearly described. "There is a logic for testing theories but no logic for creating them; there are no recipes for making original discoveries. Even attempts to identify scientific creativity in terms of specific abilities or character traits have had limited success. . . . Many creative ideas have occurred unexpectedly in an intuitive flash," [2] writes Ian Barbour, himself a physicist. The idea of the Gestalt is sometimes used to describe what happens when a new hypothesis is "born": a new structuring of perception has taken place.

Scientists form into communities and act corporately. They build on theories from the past, they perfect experiments through mutual checking, and they are stimulated through the discussion and criticism of peers. *The Double Helix,* the story of the discovery of the molecular structure of genes (DNA), is a dramatic presentation of scientists at work.[3] It indicates that the scientific community has its own body of attitudes and traditions within which members operate. Scientists have their own paradigms, develop their own analogues and models and use a language couched in its own symbols. The basic philosophy undergirding scientific work is realism; that is, scientists assume that their theories represent real events in the world. Their work is not simply to observe and record but to make intelligible and rational.

> The scientific enterprise, in summary, is a *many-faceted phenomenon*. Its genius has been precisely the interaction of components which oversimplified accounts have portrayed in isolation. It involves both logical processes and a creative imagination transcending logic. . . . Individual activity and originality are significant but occur within the tradition of a scientific community and under the influence of its paradigms.[4]

The empirical method is approached philosophically through the development within epistemology of linguistic analysis. Philosophers are recognizing the existence of many "languages" within language, each of which is descriptive of a particular mode of inquiry. Science has its language; theology has a language. Sometimes the two fields use the same words, with similar or divergent meanings. The functions and the uses of language differ. Scientific language is used to understand the world in particular ways. Religious language may be related to the formation of attitudes, the development of a way of life, the expression of worship, or the evocation of commitment.[5] Such acceptance of the distinctiveness of language use obviates the sense of competition or conflict between the fields of science and religion insofar as each serves a different function. Theology, as well as science, has a cognitive aspect; assertions are made in belief, ethics, and worship. Both fields seek truth and understanding. Religious beliefs are based on experiential and historical data, use models, and interpret through concepts. They seek a pattern of coherence. There are similarities and contrasts in the two approaches. Religious scholars today are not interested in "natural theology," nor in ignoring nature; rather, they seek "a *theology of nature* that can preserve the distinctive contributions of both science and religion." [6]

Langdon Gilkey has pointed out that the neo-orthodox position, while denouncing traditional natural theology, nevertheless assumed the scientific view of the world. This is indicated, first, by saying that historical events could be seen as revelatory of God's action only as viewed through eyes of faith, and second, by assuming that events proceeded in chronological (historical) order. He writes, "They desacralized or demythologized that scientific picture of an evolving universe, and tried to keep it separate from their theology." [7]

Religious people bring the scientific world view and some form of the empirical method into the church. Children absorb this world view from their earliest educational experiences. Science enters the curriculum in the nursery school. Highly educated people live within the framework of empirical method. "Show me, demonstrate, prove it" are internalized attitudes of the Western world.[8] Holders of the most conservative of Christian positions will assert that they can prove the truth of the Bible, the reliability of tradition, or the activity of God.

Some aspects of empirical method give the assurance of stability in the face of change. This has happened three times within the past four hundred years: in Galileo's restructuring of accepted views of the relationship of earth to sun, in Darwin's restructuring of views of the relationship of humans to other creatures, in Einstein's restructuring the view of the relationship of matter to energy. The educational responsibility that the church has toward its people is to use the empirical method for facing facts, to look critically at how attitudes are developed, to have a rationale for their ethic, and to understand the dynamics of belief and worship. The bases of religious faith are enlarged through this kind of perspective. The scientist's respect for observation and reticence in drawing conclusions should commend itself to the Christian who supposedly cultivates humility and discernment. A trend toward operational goals for education brings a degree of specificity that reflects an empirical outlook.[9]

Another aspect of empirical method that should commend itself educationally is the creative thinking implied in the use of the hypothesis—the freedom to guess and seriously to consider the possibilities suggested by an observation. The flash of insight has always commended itself to religious people as a possible work of the Holy Spirit.[10] The worlds of meaning opened up by persistent scientific inquiry, from the invisibility of atoms to the equivalent invisibility of the far reaches of space, evokes the sense of awe and wonder, which has always been a component of worship and of faith.

The scientific world view and methodology can contribute to the church's task of helping people face change. The interpretative function of scientific inquiry can bring reassurance. The breadth of the findings can put the particulars of change into a new perspective; the terrible powers unleashed by atomic fission and the potential power revealed in the heat and light of uncounted stars dwarf all human powers, no matter how immediate the threat of the latter. The power of God revealed in the universe is promise of his final judgment and victory. A knowledge of the natural world, at least as much as a knowledge of history, points toward eschatology.

THE BIOLOGICAL SCIENCES: LIFE?

Through biology the minute end of the spectrum of science is disclosed. The most startling scientific discoveries have centered around breaking the genetic code and the efforts to discover how life develops. The findings are so elaborate as to verge on the fantastic. The construction of genes through the DNA molecule is such that the four nucleotides (the "letters" of the DNA "code") can be recombined into an incredible number of "sentences" carrying the "instructions," the genetic information for the development of all forms of life.

Will this make it possible to change the instructions and so develop the new person according to the will of a parent or of a community? Beneficently used, this knowledge could mean eliminating the distortions of body or mind that sometimes are present from birth. Malevolently used, it could make possible the development of people designed for special tasks. This is the nightmare that was envisaged by George Orwell in *Animal Farm* years before the DNA discovery was made. Would it be possible to grow living creatures outside the host body of the mother—or to fertilize an ovum outside and implant it for development? The implications for ethics, for family life, and for the respective roles of men and women are so far-reaching that few are interested in exploring them until the necessity arises.

Biology is involved in new life through still another avenue of development: research into fertility. Experiments with hormones have made it possible to overcome infertility and have been instrumental in blocking fertility. The "pill" has already had far-reaching effects and raised ethical questions. Natural methods of population control have been largely eliminated (maternal death, childhood diseases, famine, tuberculosis in young adults), and other methods must be used if the human race is not to crowd itself into physical and mental disaster. Ethical questions arise when such control is insistently advocated for the poor with only passing reference to the privileged.

Fertility drugs have already caused a reorientation of sexual mores within Western nations. The "double standard," long accepted as the basis for Christian morality, has virtually disappeared. When chastity can no longer be defined as it has been traditionally, what becomes the place and purpose of coitus as expressive of the relationship between men and women? New customs develop a new rationale, for people act first and then develop reasons to justify their actions.

Another aspect of changed attitudes toward sexuality is indicated by the structure and function of the family. Family life has taken many forms to meet basic social needs such as economic support, emotional support, and the nurture of children.[11] When men and women find equal job opportunities there will be no necessary economic dependence but a continuing need to provide security to those women who make nurturing children a primary work. Children are being raised outside the traditional Western form of home in Israeli *kibbutzim*, and the Society of Brothers (Bruderhof) in the United States, as well as in extended natural families.

The life sciences are also engaged in efforts to prolong life. A network of machines can keep people artificially alive when they would otherwise have died. The improvement of skills in making organ transplants has given new life to many people. Several kinds of questions arise. One question is that of the wisdom of weighting the population toward the aged by increasing longevity while decreasing births. Another question concerns the basis on which the expensive mechanisms for prolonging life are administered: financial ability, skills needed by society, or family need? A newspaper carried the story of a young man kept alive for three years on a kidney machine. During each interval out of the hospital this young man was engaged in lawbreaking activities. Perplexed doctors pondered the dilemma of withholding the machine from a more "worthy" citizen or deliberately permitting a human death. The young man made the decision: he absented himself too long and died.

When dying was removed from the home and from religious traditions and taken into the hospital, the medically oriented people there, dedicated to saving life, saw death as failure and defeat. Thus the questions which the biological sciences raise are ethical. This is why the religious dimension is so important and the educative work of the church essential.[12] The religious community has resources to help people understand their own death and that of others. The Lord of Christian life died a real death before he was raised from the dead. The Bible is filled with situations in which death, violent or natural, took place, where life was prolonged or shortened. The resources of faith are to enable people to accept mortality.

When the church's attitude toward change is considered, it

is seen to revolve around those discoveries of biological science that have led to what is known as the sexual revolution. But there is no Biblical prescription on this score. Bathsheba and David, Gomer, the women forgiven by Jesus—these were examples given to illustrate the grace of God. The reality of the present situation has caused some ethicists to move from a morality of principle into a morality of context. Most resist a situational ethic as being too flexible to give stable guidelines for societal well-being. The teachers of religion, theologians, and pastors are in a dilemma. The tide of sexual morality has turned. Efforts to hold to a Biblical pattern, structured into the Christian style of life, may become an archaic hope. This may be a pendulum swing or a new attitude developing between men and women, toward marriage and the family. Religious people are aware of being caught in the midst of a change that calls into question their whole belief as to what constitutes right living for adults in a basic area of existence. Prescriptions for societal living set forth two thousand years ago do not interest the young and are ignored by many of their elders. Preaching and teaching in any rational way will not bring about the desired result. Models of alternative lifestyles, joyfully Christian and fully human, would be helpful. If love can endure for many years between the same two persons, if mutual fidelity can be a strengthening, supportive factor in life, then this must be demonstrated. If children can enrich a marriage instead of straining it, this too must be demonstrated. Full and open discussion with mutual forbearance is the only way by which unity can be sustained within the Christian community. If people feel that they are being judged, but at the same time do not feel guilty, they will avoid the group that has seemingly excluded them.

To the Stars

While biological sciences have explored the most minute elements of life, astrophysics has had eyes, and cameras, on the outer reaches of space. This is a breathtaking view of the universe inhabited by humankind. The mind cannot quite encompass galaxies beyond galaxies where the light that reaches earth left a sun thousands of years ago. Suddenly the solar system seems small and its exploration seems possible. A trip to the moon no longer keeps people fascinated before a television screen. Only the first look was wonderful. Curiosity has now been satisfied. Now let us explore Mars and Venus! Human creatures begin to hope that there may be other living beings, comparable to themselves, in some other solar system. Intricate equipment explores space by sight and sound for evidences that someone in the universe is trying to get in touch with us. Earth has become small, but the universe has enlarged almost infinitely; suddenly the human creature feels small, alone. The words of Psalm 8—"What is man, that thou art mindful of him? And the son of man, that thou visitest him?"—now have a poignant ring. The question is asked not so much in wonder but in hope of the assurance that indeed there is someone to be mindful of him.

Faced with this kind of world (or worlds), no wonder space travel gives a certain comfort. If one can fly around the earth at a fast pace, the next step is to fly beyond earth. The dreams of utopia begin to cluster around the moon—which has been the object of fantasies for a long time. Stanley Kubrick's movie, *2001: A Space Odyssey,* caught the mood: the coldly efficient space station (just like an international airport), where people of many nations met in passing, the smooth silence of the spaceship itself. Then, the fantasy quality of this "other world." Reality has been exhausted, to be replaced by the dream. Just in time has come the geodesic dome, invented by the fertile mind of Buckminster Fuller. The coziness of enclosed space can simulate earth atmosphere on the gray expanses of the lunar landscape. Are these hopes, illusions, or an escape from the pervasive problems of earthly existence? Europeans in the seventeenth and eighteenth centuries came to the Western Hemisphere and found unspoiled land on which to settle, the original inhabitants having taken good care of the land. Nineteenth- and twentieth-century Europeans and Asiatics could still view America as a land of opportunity. Now there is no place to flee. One must make a new life in one's own country or think about distant worlds. Like the view from the spaceship, the satellite view of earth is one of green earth, blue water, and passing clouds. It is beautiful, the astronauts exclaim. But earthbound people are so close they see the ugliness.

The astronaut, through the veil of space, sees earth as it might have been at the creation, or in the long aeons before the last ice age receded and humans began to establish dominion. The reflection of this view of earth evokes two responses: the myth of the eternal return to some earlier Eden or the hope of some future perfect kingdom—the new Jerusalem. The response to the possibility of change is a search for the familiar.

Whether one leans toward a big bang theory of creation, or a view of a continuously expanding universe, it is certain that no one has a final answer to this searching question. The struggle between science and religion has passed in the realization that each story is a response to a different question. The vastness of interstellar space evokes the questions of teleology: what is the end of man? what is the purpose of human existence? These are metaphysical or religious questions. To have them separated from scientific questions is a gain. They can be better considered within the framework of the nature of faith, theistic or humanistic. Sometimes the impression is left that the church considers such questions peripheral. Human beings seem vulnerable in their small spaceships. No wonder they ask where they are going. And the questions about God persist. It may be, as Tillich, and Robinson, following him, would suggest,[13] that God is neither "down," nor "in," nor "out there," but "around." The understanding of God as creator has become enlarged beyond measure so that "creation" subsumes not simply our small solar system, nor even our vast galaxy, but myriad galaxies. The more personal questions of the relationship between God and his people need to be answered within this context or they cannot be fully satisfying. This is an intellectual task of the church in its teaching ministry: both to explore and to help others explore the meaning of God in a century when astrophysics flourishes.

The Ultimate Power: Atomic Energy

Power and change as keynotes in contemporary existence are surely epitomized in the reality of atomic energy, which alternately promises to improve and threatens to destroy life.

This amazing source of power springs from an infinitesimal source. When the terrible fact of the destruction of Hiroshima burst upon this nation, the soothing assurance was given that within a decade all the cities of earth would be lighted by atomic energy, and all the factories in the world, fueled with atomic energy, would produce goods enough to wipe out poverty and deprivation. This was a false hope. The quest for the many uses of atomic energy is epitomized in that medium-sized community set off the road by itself—Oak Ridge, Tennessee. It may have a higher percentage of Ph.D.'s than any other community in the country and most of its people work in town—or, one should say, "out of town," for the place where people live has to be protected from the places where they work. Everyone wears an identification card with a Geiger counter. Some buildings, off base to visitors, arouse the ominous thought that this might be where the bombs are made. Elsewhere, in towering buildings with unbelievably complicated machinery and processes, the magic fuel is developed by manufacturing fissionable material. The human mind can scarcely comprehend how all this equipment could be needed for preparing a few ounces (or even a few pounds) of material. Much less can one imagine the power locked in those few ounces. One learns of cancer research but hears little of cures; one sees films of vast earth-digging operations and then learns that these cannot become operative because it seems impossible to decontaminate the earth thus prepared for building. A strange community of hard-driving energy, complete dedication, golden hopes, and ambiguous results.

At the moment, atomic energy is largely a promise. Some entire communities where the cement foundations of houses contain atomic leavings have been found inimical to health. Around the country, the desperate desire for more electrical power vies with the fear that atomic energy plants will pollute water, land, and air.

Over all hangs anxiety about what will happen if nations start hurling atomic weapons. The threat of global annihilation infects earth. Perhaps literally the meek will inherit the earth: the "haves" will destroy each other's technological culture and the "have nots" alone will be left to carry on the human race. The new science necessitates a new brand of diplomacy. It may even require a new kind of human being who is less driven by his own aggressiveness and need for power. Ridiculous thought! No test tube is ready to make this baby.

For the most part, people of earth have become resigned to the threat of the bomb, despite continual massive testing. At most, they are annoyed by the money being spent and the fear of fallout. No longer are shelters popular or air raid drills carried on in schools. The people who feel the inertia are those in the electric companies who fight every inch of the way for new generators. They feel that change is being blocked irrationally.

How, then, does the church deal with a promise that has overtones of making people more fully human and undertones of destroying the earth? How can this source of power be viewed as beneficent? What is the task of the church in a community where the use of atomic energy is a life issue? In dealing with this, as with other scientific issues, the church can avoid a stand, block change, or direct change. (The impressive church buildings at Oak Ridge speak eloquently of the financial status of their scientific membership.) What is the proclamation of the gospel in such a situation? What is the form of social action?

THE CHURCH'S TASK

The physical sciences have made great strides in the twentieth century, posing questions that the Christian community must consider seriously. In its teaching ministry, the church has a task to inform people, to help them make decisions, to encourage them to become involved in the events of community life. The scientific work of the world is done by the laity. They are proclaiming the faith and the Christian style of life. If the church avoids the issues of change (which increasingly are ethical issues), it ceases to clarify issues and give guidance. Then the scientific community—and most of the laity, whose education is grounded in empirical method—will become indifferent. If the church truly grapples with the problems and frankly takes a stand with good reason, it might at least win the respect of the nonchurched. The church cannot opt out of the social scene. It will not always be right, and it may sometimes be trying to hold back a tide. But what it must do is to indicate its convictions by its corporate life and the life of its people. This is the task of Christian education in a culture permeated by the scientific approach to life.

Chapter 4

Science Applied:
The Uses of Technology

THERE has always been technology. Stone Age people made implements. Ethnological museums are filled with artifacts thousands of years old. Why, then, the sudden apprehension about technology? The Luddites made their famous protest in the early 1800's, trying to stop the introduction of the power looms, which they feared would take away their jobs. What actually happened was that mass-produced materials at lower prices generated more business and increased the number of available jobs. The question, still unsettled, is whether the life of the worker was improved. That unsuccessful protest has remained in memory, uncomfortably haunting the Western world as industrial development increased. It reappears in a newspaper article entitled "The Luddites Were Not All Wrong," in which a professor of economics insists that the quality of life has been steadily deteriorating and that people have the right and the necessity to decide when technology is good and should be developed and when it is destructive and should not be followed further.[1]

Langdon Gilkey says that "technology itself has become one of the fates that haunt modern man, mocking his control over himself and even over nature. In fact, it has almost replaced blind nature as the main causative factor in whatever threatens our contemporary existence."[2] He continues by outlining the ways in which he sees this illustrated:

Technology has the character of fate because the *fact* of the development or further expansion of technology cannot be stopped and is thus quite beyond human control. The *shape* or *direction* of this unstoppable expansion is also not under any measure of rational determination or control. The development and use of technology reveals itself to be the servant . . . of our more sinful or greedy impulses—of the profit motive, of national pride, and of national or class paranoia.[3]

Technology both puts humankind in bondage and expresses man's bondage. It reinforces whatever deterministic forces are already in the environment.

TECHNOLOGY AND PEOPLE

Norbert Wiener, the "father" of modern cybernetics, also sees the dangers of this force let loose on earth. His brief lectures entitled *God and Golem, Inc.* are subtitled *A Comment on Certain Points Where Cybernetics Impinges on Religion.*[4] The name Golem refers to the medieval legend of the rabbi who saved his life by displaying magical powers obtained by bargaining with God. The conflict comes with some internal feeling that it is improper to devote unusual powers to selfish purposes. The sin of sorcery haunts humans even when they no longer believe in God. Technology has made it possible to obtain a wish before knowing fully what the consequences will be. The results can be catastrophic. So the ethical questions cannot be left to the machine or made by humans without reference to technology, but rather through the human use of cybernetics.

If the computer were simply a storage space for information, it would be a welcome relief to the overtaxed human brain at a time when there is too much information available. But machines have not been made that can be programmed to draw deductions from information and to make decisions. People find this comforting when it means monitoring the sick or sounding an alarm when a balance is disturbed. It becomes awesome when the machines go into action to solve complex problems posed by astronauts in space. It becomes disquieting when the computers weigh the military capabilities of fellow nations and draw conclusions for military decisions. A machine does not react emotionally, but the information given evokes emotional responses in the humans who read the print-outs. The final decisions are still made by people.

While the ethical implications of computer knowledge and decisions are of paramount importance, cybernetics has raised other issues about the effect of computers on people. Through the years, educated people have watched without too much concern while unskilled jobs disappeared, in the hope that skills were being increased so that workers were making more money at more comfortable jobs. This was not the fact. Thousands never moved to the distant city where the new factory was built, or were never able to change their work patterns in order to accept different jobs.

Now cybernetics has moved into the decision-making field. Visitors to a computer center are sometimes invited to watch a machine play checkers or golf. This is amusing until one realizes that much middle-income work involves this kind of decision. Certain given factors and limited variables form the parameters for options. An industrial society assumes that it is more efficient to hire one machine than x number of people, for the human costs are not included in the cost of a product. Highly educated and technically trained people in comfortably salaried positions lose jobs. This negates a generally held assumption that more education leads to better job security. Ironically, the only new jobs seem to be in the area of computer programming—in functions setting the "stage" by which the computer would later make the decisions.

Education was supposed to make people flexible enough to fit many jobs. Industry found that flexibility decreased with age and experience and that it was easier to train young people. Fewer people were needed. The result is that young peo-

ple stay in school longer and older workers are retired earlier.
Questions of the right to work or the need to work are an ethical concern, assuming that what happens to persons is an
important question for a society.

Technology affects the concept of work. If work ceases to
be demanding, it may also cease to be interesting. Work could
become the time each person contributes toward the productivity of a society. When both men and women work, the number of hours needed per person is reduced and so are the years
spent in financially remunerated work. Physically heavy work
disappears, and much "thinking" work also disappears. A
newly structured perception of the self will be needed in which
working is not the key role. After untold generations of believing that to work was to be an adult and not to work was to be
lazy, these terms will need reconstruction.

Other questions concern what forms the new leisure will
take, the interaction between work and leisure, and the shape
of the family with the new leisure. The nuclear family could
have more opportunity for creative interaction, with lessened
tensions concerning work, or the intimacy might reach destructive proportions. Friendships and community relationships
could be enhanced, or instead there might be more encouragement for the peripatetic longings of people; the second home
for winter and summer sports; the weekend or week in distant
places. Such bifurcation of interest makes it less likely that
people will develop a deep concern with any one place. Own-
ing two homes now makes a family inhabitants of two states,
and sometimes of two nations. The religiously oriented become
participants in two parishes. (This has been an upper-class
pattern for generations.)

The religious and educational dimension of the technological factor is enunciated by Andrew M. Greeley:

> The problem is not in technology, as some romanticists be-
> lieve, but rather in man's social, organizational, and moral
> skills. His ability to organize his activities, and his ethical
> systems, have not kept pace with his technical skills. Un-

less he is able to recapture a sense of his own oneness with
the world and his respect for its rhythms and cycles, he may
find that his triumph over it is Pyrrhic, and that he has conquered the world only to place himself in a worse bondage
to it.[5]

The religious community must help people to perceive ethical questions raised by the development of technology, such
as those of human freedom and initiative. Is all development
good? Is all "progress" really a forward step? When should
decisions be made not to continue developments, or to change
their direction or even to destroy work already accomplished?
This calls for the discussion of ethical situations with intent to
change attitudes and actions. Blowing up a computer center
will not end the use of computers, for, as the sorcerer's ap-
prentice discovered, once the magic secret is known, the product proliferates until another word is deliberately spoken to
change the action. Business ethics has not begun to deal with
such issues, even though business people have been the main-
stay of the religious establishment.

The heart of the matter lies in how human beings are perceived with reference to their place in technological society.[6]
People have always been expendable. Until this present century natural disasters and the perils of existence kept the life
expectancy low. Today physical life may continue for a long
time, but there is need to make life meaningful and give it
dignity. Religions have been concerned with persons. If the
concern is to relate persons to God as a substitute for enhancing life or to provide a palliative for the drabness of existence,
then the intent of the Western religious tradition is being denied. Both the personal experience of God and the fulfillment
of his purposes come about through life. Amos announced that
he was a herdsman as well as a prophet, and Paul insisted that
he made his living as a tentmaker as well as by being a
preacher of the gospel. The church, as it educates, should give
people the assurance of their worth. The Christian affirmation
that Christ died for each person, that God made and loves

each person, is at the very center of this kind of education.

The church's attitude toward persons finds another focus in the emergent leisure society. If the church is supposed to be active in the world, a minimal workweek should make it possible for Christians to demonstrate their life-style in a variety of ways within their communities. No longer need there be a conflict over time spent on institutional church work and time spent acting as Christians in community affairs. Christians will need to be better informed and will need to learn how to act on issues. New focal points of education are involved in such a process.

The concept of a church "home" or a neighborhood church may become weakened. Not many people are flocking to ski-slope chapels or catching a service at the airport en route to a flight. The parish long ago ceased to be a geographical boundary, and it may in the foreseeable future cease even to have a community boundary. The Catholic concept of parish as area and the Protestant concept of church as community of commitment may both be near an end. The episodic nature of religious education is already being recognized by devices such as unit courses (to hold teachers through limited "contracts"), weekday classes (when continuity on Sundays is not possible), weekend conferences, family nights, and so on.[7] When the reality of the situation finally takes hold, these and other options will be considered. For a generation, the church has tried to adjust to congregations whose members moved every few years. "We train them for the next parish" was said by clergy, more with bravado than conviction. Now, time is further telescoped. People move from weekend to weekend. What is the educational responsibility of the church to a revolving congregation?

ELECTRONICS AND THE MEDIA

Technology reaches directly into homes through television. Marshall McLuhan sensed the direction in his first and most scholarly book, *The Gutenberg Galaxy*.[8] Preliterate groups, he wrote, used to listen to stories when the group gathered together. Oral tradition was the source of information. The invention of linear type favored the production of literate folk who gathered information through reading. Much education has been programmed toward this end. The twentieth century has seen the development of people whose information comes by sound and pictures. McLuhan's later writings explore the interactions and effects of cinema and television. The latter, he says, is a "cool" medium, which one watches with an immediacy that requires that the whole self become involved. Cinema is a "hot" medium because it is so large as to envelop the viewer. He notes, however, that television techniques have influenced recent developments in film, when episodes, quick cuts, and superimposed images seem unfamiliar to longtime moviegoers but catch the awareness of the young.[9]

A whole generation has been brought up on television, but controversy still swirls around what is learned and what residual effects there are to viewing programs. One can only speak of the effects of types of programs on the groups who watch them. The power of television lies in its propinquity—it is in almost every home, and the product is available at the turn of a dial. Events come through with immediate power. Indeed, the viewer is closer than if he were part of the crowd at an event, which is why people carry transistor radios and portable television sets to football games. Television has made possible the monitor, in which a whole building can be watched from one console. Closed-circuit television makes an event available to a limited group; an assembly of doctors can watch an operation, a group of teachers can observe the playback of a class session, or children in widely separated rural communities within a state can take the same arithmetic course. But the potential has been only partially realized.

Film is a still-evolving medium, old enough to generate historical interest as well as experimentation. The director is "creative," the photographer is an artist. A film may be hours long, with an intermission, or it may be only a few minutes in length. The impact comes less through a chronological story line than through impressions in which the viewer becomes involved. Film may have as many flashbacks as the classical form of the novel. To such an extent have people become one world that films originating in Japan, Ghana, India, Italy, Sweden, and the United States may be seen and understood in many lands.

Sound has reached new dimensions through electronic amplification. A symphony orchestra can be heard with power within the concert hall, an organ has wide range in tonality and power, but the sound is still limited in comparison to that of amplified instruments. The difference is important: the new music is felt physically as well as emotionally. Young people respond to this total sound. There is wide diversity in music —from John Cage and taped music to switched-on Bach, to the latest in folk, to rock or whatever is the popular music of the moment.

When sounds and multiple projected materials are used together, the impact is all-involving. In the theater, slides may be flashed on the stage background or used for a scene setting. Film may be incorporated into the action. The interaction among media points toward diversity and flexibility in the construction of art forms.

Electronics has had an impact also on three-dimensional art. Op art has brought a mobile quality to picture and sculpture which may be an extension of what Alexander Calder did originally in the construction of mobiles. Art forms incorporate many kinds of materials, including the "found" sculptures of Pablo Picasso and the elaborate wooden constructions of Louise Nevelson. Canvasses strive for three-dimensional effects.

What will be the place of books in a pictorially oriented world? Television news spots could replace newspapers, documentaries supplant magazines, and forms of dramatic art make books superfluous. Yet movie study guides are published to facilitate reflection upon film,[10] and television documentaries become available as educational films. Some books themselves incorporate a visual approach.[11]

Books have been affected by the electronic revolution. Not only is most printing done by electronic processes, but the reproduction of printed material can be made by all sorts of copiers at minimal cost. Linear type is more prolific than ever.

The subject of copiers leads to a consideration of the hardware of learning. Movie projectors are now so simply constructed that anyone can insert the cartridge of film. Similarly filmstrips, slides on a carousel projector, tapes, cassettes, and records can be used by children for independent or small-group study.

Such technological developments are significant for the specifically educational aspects of the church's ministry. The simplistic linear story-film with the happy ending has been replaced with living, if disconcerting, situations. Filmstrips are paired with records in which sound effects are more important than interpretive text. Simultaneous use of two projectors indicates the impatience of media people with the limitations of the simpler forms of projected material. Settings for the service of worship are found in folk, pop, and rock—expressive of various cultures and many moods of music. Established musicians compose for liturgical settings. The music of Bloch and Poulenc seems traditional alongside the latest offerings of Bernstein and Penderecki. The preeminence of the organ is challenged by the use of other instruments. The artifacts of worship become newly contemporary in each decade, whether made of ceramic, silver, wool, or silk.

Education through the senses becomes basic—whether through multidimensional forms of worship or through the media used interpretatively for study. All forms that are available within a culture are suitable for the religious dimension of learning. Media may have introduced an expensive dimension, available only to the affluent. But the cost of technology is being lowered, and it seems as if this way of teaching is here to stay. The church is still learning how to use television effectively. Even the most colorful liturgical services do not move swiftly enough to hold the viewer's attention, and talk programs are seldom structured sharply enough to have impact. As McLuhan has noted of commercials in general, these have their own technique, and the religious ones may in the end be the most effective form of ecclesiastical television.[12]

EARTH AS ENVIRONMENT

Technology has had a controversial effect on the environment. The suspicion that technology might be destructive has developed slowly. A few years ago the word "ecology" was known only to a relatively small group of scholars. Now there is a general awareness that ecology points to social issues affecting the quality of life and health of all living creatures. There is grim humor in the cartoon that pictures one tree saying to another, "If they don't stop polluting the air, I'm going to stop making oxygen for them." The productivity of a factory was customarily reckoned in terms of the number of units produced in relation to unit cost. Now, the use of the environment is considered part of the cost.

One reason for the sudden concern has been increased population, related to increased affluence. Thousands of people rushing from city to country for weekends set into motion all kinds of counterproductive forces through their methods of locomotion, their forms of housing, and their activities.

Another cause for concern is the consumer-oriented culture in which everyone is encouraged to desire and acquire many things that will wear out or otherwise become obsolete in a short time. Disposable products keep the factories in production using raw materials and generating jobs. Any break in the cycle is potentially disastrous for the economic well-being of an industrialized society. The question arises: Is there a point at which industrial development has peaked, so that further refinement would bring diminishing returns in satisfactory life-styles for people?

One effect of the negative environmental conditions in the large cities has been a flight beyond the suburbs into the countryside. This has been an effort to return to a simpler life, perhaps a nostalgic approach to existence, to get away from hurry, rudeness, insistent demands, and impersonal living. The explosive tensions that build up where there are crowded conditions and poverty are endemic. Industries are locating hundreds of miles from large cities, and new suburbs are growing up in rural areas. Soon it becomes apparent that the problems are inherent in community life. In what were once villages with a few hundred inhabitants, zoning laws are established, school bonds are fought over, sewage systems raise property tax levels, and new roads destroy the picturesque quality of whole areas. Flight brings no solutions. A new life-style for industrialized people must be sought. The price of simplicity may be to give up conveniences. Is the result worth the discipline? The question has been avoided up to now except by the young who for a time, at least, have sought another way. However, their vision also is plagued by contradictions. Conservation means care: of the land, of the houses, of the people. Sports cars and high-fidelity components have their own way of adding to environmental problems. No one is exempt. No one has found real simplicity of life.

People have lived in cities since ancient times. In times of stress cities have been destroyed and abandoned and rural life has been restored to dominance, as in the Middle Ages. Creative planners are asking how cities can become truly habitable, and how new cities can be developed with life-enhancing qualities.[13]

The question of ecology hit the religious community suddenly through an article in the magazine *Science* entitled "The Historical Roots of our Ecological Crisis," by Lynn White.[14] The author asserted that Western people use the environment thoughtlessly because it is in their religious tradition to do so. In Gen., ch. 1, man is given dominion over the earth and over all created things. In contrast, the religions of the East stress the oneness of humankind with other creatures and the natural world. (It should be added that the original inhabitants of the Western Hemisphere have also believed and lived this.) The theologians protest that "dominion" means stewardship under a righteous God, who is the only Lord of creation and under whose judgment humankind stand with reference to how they live within the world. The secular world replies that formal theology does not affect the attitude that people receive from their religious heritage.

It becomes the educational task of church and synagogue so to interpret Scripture that the place of humans in God's world is rightly understood and rightly lived. The historical revelation can be stressed in such a way as to ignore the revelation in creation. This is hardly the intent of Genesis, even as the introduction to the story of Israel. It is also possible so to dwell on the good news of redemption as to minimize the significance of creation—itself a gracious act of God. What is required is a greater sense of the wholeness of Biblical revelation, manifested in story, sermon, and study.

There is also need of action through which the religious community witnesses to simplicity as a way of life. The prophets showed this. Jesus and his first followers had necessarily lived this way. The church itself, as institution, and through the building in which a congregation is housed, can witness to a way of life that demonstrates stewardship of resources. Individuals, in daily work and living, can learn to contribute to life in such a way as to respect natural resources and the other creatures with which they share the earth. This requires a methodology of action and attitude, reflecting an understanding of the relationship of people to God vis-à-vis the environment.

Part II

THE WORD: THEOLOGY

Chapter 5

Speaking About God

THE cultural setting affects how people think about and interpret their religion. The present cultural setting is characterized by change, conflict, and emphasis on power. It is engaged in futuristic thinking yet fearful of an apocalypse. Each group of people feel themselves to be a minority with respect to age, sex, race, ethnic group, or economic condition. This is a scientifically and technologically oriented world, just beginning to question the results of its own Promethean work.

The religious community constructs its own view of reality based on belief in the ultimate and consonant with its understanding of the ends of existence. The history of Christian thought indicates how specific theological trends have become the concern of the church in each period of its life. Within just a century and a half "orthodoxy" has been infiltrated by strains of liberal theology, followed by a form of orthodoxy permeated with Biblical criticism. Because of the swift succession of emphases, it is too soon to characterize the trend that will typify the end of the twentieth century. It is helpful to remember W. Norman Pittenger's explanation that "orthodoxy is not so much the using of ancient language as it is the continuing participation in the reality which that language was devised to affirm, and of course to affirm in the only idiom available at the time when the affirmation was made." [1]

The present mood is one of openness and diversity. There is freedom to interpret and little consensus among either professionals or laity. There seems to be general agreement that system-building is finished for a while. There will not soon be another Barthian *kirchliche Dogmatik* or even a modest three-volume systematic theology like Paul Tillich's. Heterodoxy, no matter how anathema to classical Christian doctrine, is the posture taken by many Christians today. In such an atmosphere what words can be spoken about God?

It is generally accepted that the change from neo-orthodoxy began with consideration of some words of Dietrich Bonhoeffer's in various letters written from prison.[2] The most influential phrases arising out of his letters are "religion in a world come of age," "religionless Christianity," and "living without a *deus ex machina*." His ideas were further popularized in a widely circulated book, *Honest to God*, by Church of England Bishop John A. T. Robinson, who delineated the thought of three theologians reflecting the post–World War II religious mentality: Tillich, Bonhoeffer, and Rudolf Bultmann.[3] Despite initial outcries from both theologians and laity of traditional faith, his insights have proved sound. The mythology of the Bible continues to obfuscate the Christian message for the educated person, to speak of a God "out there" is considered a mistake in the space age, and people seem to feel no need to have someone else save them. Whether these elements are necessary to religion and to personal life is another question.

The ultimate deductions from Bonhoeffer were made by the "death of God" theologians. In effect they said that the imagery surrounding the word "God" was untenable but that in Jesus the Western world had a figure who could give meaning to life.[4] This was an extreme reaction to the definitive categories of orthodoxy, but it aroused some positive response to the problem raised even while evoking scorn among professionals, who deemed it lacking in intellectual content. One thing is certain: theology will not be the same since the discussion they provoked. Among the giants of the preceding generation, Tillich alone continues to speak to a younger generation. If his theology is a "new liberalism," then that is the category for this period in which God is seen as the ground of being, when the existential questions of life can be answered only as they are raised, and when affirming existence is the basic stance of life.

A final note is offered by Richard L. Rubenstein, reflecting upon the holocaust of a people willing to believe through all the agony that they were the chosen people of God and that whatever happened was his doing and would eventuate in triumph. (Some might say that the rise of the nation of Israel vindicates this classic theological stance.) For himself, says Rubenstein, the only answer is atheism. He feels that if this is election, who wants it? if this is providential, who needs it? [5]

God in an Age of Unbelief

From this kind of background what positive theology could emerge? Even the religious person has become a kind of unbeliever! In effect, however, it can be said that the ground has been cleared. No longer can the theologian merely appeal to some basic understanding of the faith.

No one has seen this more clearly than Edward Schillebeeckx, a Dutch theologian who addresses himself to a people indifferent to Christianity. In a series of lectures given in the United States he traced the development of the relationship between secularization and Christian belief from the time of Augustine and pointed optimistically to the current scene.

Now, however, in a culture which is resolutely turned toward the future as something that it means to make, what has in fact come about is that the flexible Christian concept of "transcendence," which is open to more than one meaning, is also affected by this shift. "Transcendence" thus tends to acquire a special affinity for what is called, in our temporality, "future." If divine transcendence really embraces past, present, future, God will be associated with future, and since this involves all mankind and men live in community, God is associated with the future of mankind.[6]

In a later book he points out that, more than ecumenical dialogue, what is needed today is "a dialogue with the vast world of atheism; or rather, to put it more accurately, with the exponents of that form of religiousness, so widespread today, whose outlook is purely of this world."[7] Schillebeeckx is concerned with the apologetic task of theology. Elsewhere he speaks to the Christian community, reinterpreting the meaning of the Sacraments and asking how this basic form of encounter between God and man can be meaningfully interpreted for Christians to whom the old words and actions hold no meaning.[8]

Leslie Dewart, a Canadian theologian, also addresses himself to the secular Christian, as is indicated by the title of his book—*The Future of Belief: Theism in a World Come of Age.* The writings of both Tillich and Bonhoeffer form the background for his writing. Atheism is a belief in the "absence of God," and he affirms that this possibility exists only within the Judeo-Christian tradition. The phrases by which he would renew Christian theism are: not "being" or "existence," but "being present"; not "person," but "self"; not "omnipotent," but "all things possible"; "the radical openness of history"; not "eternity," but "present in history." He goes so far as to say that perhaps there will need to be new ways of speaking about God without naming him.[9]

The problems of belief today are described by Gregory Baum in the introduction to a book significantly entitled *Man Becoming: God in Secular Experience.*

A Christian meets his crisis when the spiritual experience of his culture is no longer reconcilable with the religious outlook he has inherited and God seems to be more powerfully present in the former than the latter . . . . [He needs to have] available to him theological methods by which he may discover a new unity of religious experience where the

Gospel celebrated in the church sheds light on and inten-
sifies the Spirit-created redemptive values present in the
culture to which he belongs.[10]

From this perspective Baum proceeds to look at redemption,
church, eschatology, and the doctrine of God.

Martin E. Marty, whose technical field is modern church
history, has been highly sensitive to the current belief climate.
In *The Search for a Usable Future* he says that a new theology
must be oriented toward action, directed toward a world of
sudden change, applicable and available to wide sectors of
Christians.[11] He carries this out through a selection of magazine articles collated into an annual that he edits with Dean
Peerman. In each introduction he expresses the hope that the
articles have caught the feeling of the times: successively hope,
conflict, transcendence, and so on.[12]

These speak, as did Schleiermacher in the preceding century, to religion's cultured despisers, educated persons who
feel self-sufficient without faith. Others, writing from a background of philosophical theology, make their appeal on an abstract level. Gordon R. Kaufman, beginning in his earliest
writing (1958) with a concern about existentialism, has now
put his ideas into a one-volume systematic theology.[13] Bernard
J. Lonergan's 1958 book, *Insight,* is also philosophical.[14]

One important thrust of contemporary philosophy has been
in the direction of linguistic analysis. Earlier proponents,
whose arguments stemmed from Wittgenstein, affirmed that
only declarative language made sense. Other language, including the theological and metaphysical, was tautological and
therefore non-sense. Linguistic analysis has been insistent
upon clarification of language and its use. "Philosophizing"
has never been a substitute for rigorous thinking. These philosophers are attempting to bring the rational to bear on theological discourse. The chief spokesman for the validity of religious
language has been Ian Ramsey, now bishop of Durham, England. He writes that language can be categorized by its function, and that there are many languages. Indicative words are

performative language. Religious words are commitment language.[15]

To the theologians one thing is clear: there are many people to whom Christian belief does not appeal. An earlier liberalism made sense to some, accommodating itself to the scientific outlook. The succeeding neo-orthodoxy gave an affirmative stance to a Biblical religion based on the scientific outlook, strengthening the faith of others. Catholic theologians in Europe, facing defections not only among laity but among clergy, are attempting to get at the heart of what modern people believe about life and how they are oriented in seeking goals and meaning for existence. It is not sufficient to accommodate faith to scientific knowledge; in fact, at the moment there is cynicism toward science because of its destructive potential. An appeal is made through the affirmation that life itself is good. Working at the opposite end from the Barthian thesis of the transcendent coming into human affairs, the "secular" theologian sees God as acting within the natural world which he created.

So the idea is to become aware of God where he already is. The existence of God is assumed, whether he be noticed or not. Nor is the belief only instrumental: God exists for himself and is manifested in all his works, including works that humans do through his power.

There is still no answer to the millions who find life comfortable without the theistic affirmation, nor any for those who point out the conflicts and sufferings that the religious establishment has inflicted on the world for many centuries. As Karl Rahner points out in an essay, heresy is a fact because orthodoxy is a fact, because Christianity affirms some statements to be importantly true. Any response to heresy (or to heterodoxy) must be made in response to this background.[16]

The reason these writers have favorable words for the teaching ministry is that they are hoping to win those in whom there is some residual Christianity. They remember that Jacques Maritain was a despiser in his youth; that Thomas Merton turned from secular thought to the Cistercians. They continue to believe that God made persons and that even within the hiddenness of unbelief God continues to act.

The crisis of faith must be faced seriously by the church. The golden years in which church attendance as well as enrollments soared are past. The buildings are underused; multiple worship services continue only by dint of efforts to find new formats to lend variety. Not only are young adults absent; they are keeping their children at home. It simply is not worth the trouble either to take or to send them. When nursery education begins at the age of three, not even the church kindergarten is unique.

A teaching ministry to deal with unfaith must be open. This does not mean that teachers are skeptics; on the contrary, only by having a faith to offer can they evoke the response, however negative, of those who come. Openness includes the freedom to listen, to respect the ideas of others, to remain unthreatened by criticism. The task is to understand the rationale of skepticism and of unbelief. This is not a kind of teaching for which the church has been well known.

It cannot be assumed that people are simply disillusioned with the church, either because there has been too much involvement in social issues or because the church has retreated from the world. The problem is deeper: the question of God is at the center. Either worldly involvement or transcendental meditation can be experienced "a-theistically." When the Christian resists all impulses to demonstrate or "prove" God, either as being or as existence, he will come to realize one thing. However sure he himself may be of the fact that God is revealed in events or in creation, that God is witnessed to in his own life or that of others, this fact may not be at all clear to the nonbeliever. The inquirer needs the joyous affirmation and concern of a teacher—and of the whole religious community (assuming the inquirer gets that far). The religious community is the place where the faith of the teacher is strengthened, but it is not primarily the place from which faith is witnessed to the outsider.

The new black theology is a development whereby black

Christians seek to indigenize Christian theology, applying Christian understandings to their history and their experience. Insisting that classical theology has been white and Western while claiming to be universal, they are asking if it is a viable religious option for them. Black theologians compose a wide spectrum. Albert B. Cleague, Jr., has developed his own theological system based on a "black Christ." James H. Cone sees theology in terms of helping to free people. Joseph R. Washington, Jr., has looked at the sociological roots of the black church in terms of the authority and cohesive power it has had among people. Major Jones interprets theology of hope, not eschatologically but in terms of hope for the living future. J. Deotis Roberts finds the note of reconciliation within Christian theology as one that holds promise for healing today.[17]

Asian theologians are only beginning to become free of European models. Christianity is growing rapidly in African countries, developing its own forms, which will find theological expression. It is time for an American theology to grow out of the four-hundred-year-old American culture, less dependent on the latest word from Europe (which has never really been heard by the parishes anyway).[18] Black theologians, bringing serious effort to the task in behalf of their people, may be pointing a new direction for Americans throughout the hemisphere.

GOD IN THE WORLD

To a generation to whom the Biblical world seems strange, it is useless to proclaim that God is known through these historical events. Those looking toward the future care little about the past unless they can see the continuity. The social stresses of the 1950's and 1960's evoked the affirmation that God was acting for good through the conflicts and sufferings of people.

Two streams of theology coalesce here. Teilhard de Chardin, a paleontologist and Jesuit priest, had constructed an elab-

orate system, affirming that while God is himself and therefore separate from his creation, he is at the same time completely involved in his world, so that creation is always continuing.[19] This doctrine has been termed "panentheism" in
contradistinction to the other classical philosophical position
of pantheism, which made God part of and inseparable from
the world. This is a subtle distinction, perhaps, but one that
maintains the Christian sense of the distinctive oneness of God
the Creator. Teilhard's ecclesiastical superiors were suspicious
of the distinction and he was for many years forbidden by
them to publish his books. Much of his output was released
by friends after his death in 1950. In his best-known book,
The Divine Milieu, he affirms that there can be no separation
between science and religion, between the spiritual life and
everyday life, for *all* the world is the environment in which
God acts and where Christ is encountered. Spiritual energy
divinizes all human activities. Redemption involves the whole
cosmos. Teilhard quotes from Paul: "The creation itself will be
set free from its bondage" (Rom. 8:21) and "He is before all
things, and in him all things hold together" (Col. 1:17). Christ
is the Omega Point, the culmination of creation and redemption. Teilhard, who was involved in the discovery of some of
the earliest relics of prehistoric man in China, saw God's continuing creative action through the evolutionary process.[20]

Another understanding of God viewed through the world
comes through process theology, which we first encounter in
the concept of the *élan vital* in the French philosopher Henri
Bergson. The American fountainhead was the writing of the
English-born Harvard professor Alfred North Whitehead,[21]
the succession passing to Charles Hartshorne and a group who
became known as the "Chicago School." [22] Without using Teilhard's cosmogony, they affirm that God can be known through
his work, which is his continuing activity in the world of nature and of men. The appeal of such thought could lie partly
in the tendency of Americans, having so brief a history, to be
ahistoric; hence, finding God in the Bible, while plausible to

the devout, seemed useless to a freethinking generation. Process theology made Christian faith a viable option to people who had given up a conservative past. Understandably, it again becomes an option to a generation that has given up the careful constructions of neo-orthodoxy with its distinctions between *Historie* and *Geschichte*.

Alfred North Whitehead spoke to the twentieth century because he could accept both religion and the scientific outlook and because in the secular he saw implications for the religious. He was aware that man is part of his culture but has longings for eternity. In his most definitive book he writes:

> God and the World stand over against each other, expressing the final metaphysical truth that appetitive vision and physical enjoyment have equal claim to priority in creation. But no two actualities can be torn apart: each is all in all. Thus each temporal occasion embodies God and is embodied of God.[23]

The past remains an element in the present and so becomes a part of the future. Reality is this total process—governed by God. Human life within the context of society is also part of this process and strives toward participation in a creative whole.

Whitehead's contemporary apologist is John B. Cobb, Jr. The title of his book, *A Christian Natural Theology*,[24] indicates where he wishes to go beyond Whitehead. Accepting the cosmology of the philosopher, he interprets God from the perspective of the community of faith and he acknowledges Jesus as the one to whom our lives are opened. Hence, the one who is in the process is himself the Lord who is acknowledged as functioning and made known in the world.

Schubert M. Ogden is another process thinker. He began with studies of Bultmann, indicating a concern with making the gospel understandable today. Rejecting Bultmann's reliance on Heidegger, Ogden turns to Whitehead and Hartshorne, through whose thought he believes he can speak meaningfully about God. He understands the reality of God as the central theological problem today. He thinks that the contemporary believer can accept an understanding of God as continuously involved in the world and human beings as vitally a part of this process of creation.[25]

Here is a theology for the space age. The final disentanglement from the three-story universe had to come with the first moon walk. As the giant telescopes photograph galaxies beyond galaxies, the question of God can no longer be tied to the question of human history, certainly not to events of only four thousand years past. Where Teilhard began to glimpse the age of humankind, the present generation of theologians glimpses the extent of the universe. Process theology speaks to a people who take pictures of Mars, project views of more distant planets and envision space travel in which time moves backward. Cobb has written:

> The dissolution of the physical into energy-events does not solve the question as to how we should think of God, but it should at least cause us to give up the still widely held notion that only what is physical in the naïve sense is real. It would be truer to say that what is physical in the naïve sense is the by-product of the interaction of energy-events outside the body with those that constitute the sense organs. That God is not physical in this way by no means reduces his actuality.[26]

If theistic religion is to be a viable option for the twenty-first century, the scope will need to become widened. How is it possible to speak of God, and more particularly to understand God in any kind of personal terms, when time and space have become so extended and so enlarged?

IMPLICATIONS OF PROCESS THEOLOGY FOR TEACHING

The religious emphasis turns on the human responsibility to find a place in the natural world with reference to the rights of other creatures. It means accepting creaturehood. In the first chapter of Genesis man is given dominion over all creatures—even to the extent of naming each one. It was suggested earlier in this book that this does not mean usurping the place of God as Lord, but of being a trustee of earth. The process theologians put this in more dynamic terms: humans are part of creation and participate in the continuing work of creation. This is what they are ordained to do, and this is what God is doing. If they destroy, they become demonic, a force working against God's continuing good action. They have turned away from God and no longer participate in true reality.

Ecology as a social concern paired with process as a religious concern indicates a role for humans as creatures. When a people understand their God to be part of the natural world, they are careful lest they destroy or hurt the divine and thereby bring wrath upon themselves. Western religions, not making this identification, have been careless, having neither respect nor reverence for less powerful members of creation. In the use of sheer power, their people have subjugated whatever parts of earth they have inhabited. This has reinforced their own belief in the uses of power. There is a need for a form of religious faith that can cause a rethinking of this element in the philosophy of moderns. Those who do not hesitate to use power over one another will only be restrained when they are convinced that their use of power, far from enhancing their lives, threatens to cause their death.

Process theology is a positive view of God present in creation, but it seems to lack a necessary ingredient of judgment. The Biblical tradition does not assume that the process of creation will culminate in a perfect order except through the intervention of God's judgment. It is possible that human beings, by deliberately choosing to use demonically the power with which God has endowed them, will accomplish only their own destruction. Redemption, restoration, and completion are possible only as the power of God is invoked beneficently.[27]

Process theology speaks to a generation constantly aware of

change and becomes a way by which to make sense of change. The church needs to be free enough to accept this position in its teaching along with a more traditional orthodoxy. Such heterodoxy requires flexibility in interpretation and this is a way by which the skeptical secular person might be willing to entertain any notion of God.

Process theology is helpful further by bringing a cosmic dimension to the concerns of power, conflict, and self-determination. Human beings are participants in a universe (even a multiverse). There is conflict so distant that the awareness of it is measured in aeons. Creatures on earth partake of divine power, which Christian faith has always referred to as the Holy Spirit. Parts of the liturgy have pointed in this direction: eighteenth- and nineteenth-century hymns such as "The Spacious Firmament on High," many of the Biblical psalms, and the introductory section of the Eucharistic canon giving thanks for creation and redemption.

Changes of direction in theological thinking are slow to be interpreted at the parish level in sermon, curricular materials, or study groups. The abstruse nature of theological writing does not hasten the process. The basic message of new ways of thinking about God for the educational task is that there needs continuously to be openness to seek, to share, and to reflect. Interpretations of a late-twentieth-century generation and the accumulated witness of the Christian community in Scripture and tradition need always to be seen in context with each other.[28]

Chapter 6

Witness to God

WHEN the theological climate shifts to an emphasis on the revelation of God in the world, there is a corresponding inquiry into the understanding of Jesus with reference to this knowledge of God. In the current scene, this began with the "death of God" theologians for whom Jesus became the replacement for God. The kenosis motif was developed: he is the "man for others"; in his death we have life; because he died we must continue his work and become participants in his saving mission. There are elements here of Albert Schweitzer's scholarship in an earlier generation, stripping nineteenth-century accretions from the story, recapturing the apocalyptic tones of the Gospels, and asking, Did he fail—or did he succeed?

Another strand in Christological studies stems from Rudolf Bultmann, whose brief essay began a controversy not easily stopped.[1] Bultmann insisted that because the core of the gospel is so important, the mythological elements must be stripped away so that the existential meaning is revealed. Heidegger provides the basis for his philosophy: only through an awareness of the basic questions of existence can one come to a knowledge of Christ. Moderns, Bultmann said, do not understand ancient myths and cannot hear the truth these are trying to tell. The crux of his assertions lay in his handling of the resurrection, interpreted as the new life, emphasizing the continued presence of Christ with his people.

Schubert Ogden, who translated one Bultmann book and who spent a year at Marburg where Bultmann taught, has studied this position in his book *Christ Without Myth*.[2] His main objection is to the existentialist base for the interpretation of Christ, which he finds too easily secularized. He agrees that Jesus' proclamatory word confronts us in terms of a personal response. The eternal Thou is personally present in him. This, rather than what Jesus says as teacher, is the core and must not be obscured by the myth that has developed around his person and work.

Demythologizing brought a whole new scope to studies in the life of Jesus. The post-Bultmannian developments were outlined by an American scholar who had followed them closely through the pupils of Bultmann—James M. Robinson—in *A New Quest for the Historical Jesus*.[3] The basic work to come from this period was Günther Bornkamm's study.[4] Recognizing the impossibility of developing a chronological "life" he began with information about Jesus recognizable from the earliest strata of tradition, including kerygmatic and confessional statements. The succeeding chapters outline the work of Jesus as: the proclamation of the Kingdom, the teaching of the new righteousness, the meaning of discipleship, the passion, the Messianic question, and the understanding of Jesus Christ through the resurrection, the church, and the confessions of faith.[5] The book is a serious effort to capture a description of Jesus as he was known in his time while recognizing that he can only be interpreted through the tradition that proclaimed him Lord.

CHRIST AS THE FUTURE OF GOD

Wolfhart Pannenberg, a decade later, entered the area of Christology, as indicated by the title of his book, *Jesus—God and Man*. His thesis is that the reality of the resurrection is the foundation on which Christology is built. This is the ground of Christ's unity with God, the focus of the church's preaching and the basis of its confession of faith. The resurrection, he states, was not only of visions of Jesus' disciples but also of appearances of the resurrected Jesus.[6] Setting aside so-called scientific arguments, Pannenberg affirms that the disciples spoke metaphorically, as we also must speak; and that their proclamation was made with a sense of belonging to the new age. He then considers the tradition of the empty tomb as one parallel to the Pauline tradition of appearances and indicates his assurance that this is a reliable tradition too emphatically preserved to be summarily set aside.

> If the appearance tradition and the grave tradition came into existence independently, then by their mutually complementing each other they let the assertion of the reality of Jesus' resurrection, in the sense explained above, appear as historically very probable, and that always means in historical inquiry that it is to be presupposed until contrary evidence appears.[7]

Pannenberg is more concerned with historicity than with demythologizing.

The theological thrust that seems most persistent today is the theology of hope. This emphasis began with Jürgen Moltmann's book by that name, in which he asserted that "eschatology is not one element of Christianity but the eschatological outlook is characteristic of all Christian preaching, even the existence of the whole church."[8] The revelation of God is in his promises, not in his appearance. The promise made in the past has always been kept and this is the assurance that the unfulfilled promise will be completed in God's time. Moltmann uses the Biblical image of the nomadic people, always pressing forward toward a promised, but not yet fulfilled, goal. This is salvation history. The Christian has always participated in the resurrection of Christ by obedience and by hope in the final resurrection. Christian eschatology, says Moltmann, is "Christology in an eschatological perspective."[9]

Moltmann writes out of the post-Bultmannian eschatological understanding of Christology, but carries this beyond a doctrine of Christ. The theology of hope becomes the basis for a whole school of theologizing in which the future becomes the important factor.[10] This is in tune with the prevailing futuristic studies which, it was suggested earlier, occupy scholars in many fields in looking toward developments of the year 2000. It should be quickly added that Moltmann is not setting a time for the *eschaton!* In fact, the idea of hope rather than of design may be the distinction between Christian and secular projections.

Hope has eschatological overtones of a new heaven and a new earth. A look at the beginning of the Christian church uncovers the varied ways that people hoped toward the future. It was a time of revolution—as is the twentieth century. The theologians of hope have begun to develop a theology of revolution. Moltmann picks up the theme in *Religion, Revolution, and the Future.* Lest anyone should think he means the word "revolution" in a radical sense, he says: "Radical Christianity will have a revolutionary effect, but a revolutionary program would be just the way to neutralize it. The title 'revolutionary' must, if at all, be given from outside; one cannot claim it for himself." [11]

Johannes Metz, at Münster, applies the theology of hope specifically to political theology. Because the church hopes in the future promised by God, it must become involved in the structures through which change can be realized. In his introduction to a *Concilium* volume, *Faith and the World of Politics,* he says: "Political theology seeks to make contemporary theology once again aware of the suit pending between the eschatological message of Jesus and the reality of political society. The salvation proclaimed by Jesus is permanently concerned with the world." [12] He understands the critical function of the church to be the assertion that no political system is absolute, and the mission of the church to be the interpretation of the Christian understanding of love.[13]

These European thinkers have been stimulated by Ernst

Bloch, the Marxist philosopher who has been carrying on conversation with Christians for mutual understanding—a breakthrough in which the Catholic Church has been active. The theology of revolution is also seen in the writings of two Americans, Thomas W. Ogletree and Richard Shaull.[14] It is generally recognized that the world is in the midst of a technological revolution, but it is not often asked whether this will add to or detract from human freedom. In the Christian experience of death and resurrection there is the potential for freeing people to accept change, and to help those who have had no future become participants in their new future.

Such views of Jesus and his meaning for us are scarcely apparent in liturgies or in standard church teaching. They fit neither the orthodox, liberal, nor neo-orthodox understandings of Christ. In this they illustrate the thesis that there is a plurality of ways in which basic Christian interpretations are being made today. Since these interpreters quote Scripture to verify their statements, as did the generations before them, no one can hide within Biblical teaching to escape their view of Jesus. The arts have scarcely caught up with this vision, although cinema has begun to look at an eschatological Christ.[15]

The eschatological view of Christ is not new. Yet the persistence with which this discomforting view is avoided, indicates the degree to which the church, through varied teaching options, can let people ignore what they do not like. The liturgy holds this promise in the anamnesis, which is at the heart of the Eucharist; but in some practice the idea of the joyful banquet in which the Lord is present among his people obscures the promise of his coming again in judgment, just as the memorial view in its way concentrated on the past. The Scripture lessons sometimes voice the eschatological note.

A theology of hope sounds superficially optimistic until it is realized that the "hope" lies in God's judgment and the consummation of his Kingdom. Christians pay lip service to having the new life, but few live toward death as if they believed in eternal life. The teaching task begins with the participation in the liturgy, in the preaching from the gospel and in the willingness to take risks both in personal life, in the corporate life of the church, and as members of the community, so that, as the prophets declared, justice may be made manifest. The teaching is in the doing by a committed people who take risks. This is easy to prescribe but difficult to accomplish, as the stresses within the Christian churches reveal.

THE BIBLE AS THE WORD OF GOD'S ACTION

While it is basic to the Christian faith to see in Scripture the record of God's revelatory acts, this is not usually assumed to be the only area of his self-disclosure. The emphasis on the Bible makes Christianity a historical religion, in that certain attestable events become witnesses to God's action. Catholic Christianity has carried the witness of events beyond the Biblical period into the tradition of the church. It has also acknowledged the revelation of God in the natural world, which some Protestant views accept and others reject. The revelational quality of events is known only to those who view them by faith. The same events, written in the records of others involved, such as the Babylonians or the Romans, do not carry this quality.

The first challenge to this viewpoint came in an article by Langdon Gilkey, "Cosmology, Ontology and the Travail of Biblical Language," in which he pointed out that the Biblical theologians are caught in a contradiction: through the use of scholarly tools, they can authenticate the historicity of events, yet for theological purposes they want to give a different meaning to history, inventing a category for "eyes of faith." [16] Gilkey's article seems to have marked the end of an era. The achievements have been carefully documented in a book by Brevard S. Childs that summarizes the movement: *Biblical Theology in Crisis*. The unity of the Bible began to give way and there appeared to be an openness for looking at its diversity. Childs writes:

One can hardly avoid the impression that the concentration on the elements of demonstrable distinctiveness was basically a form of modern apologetic, which, like the medieval proofs for the existence of God, maintains its validity only among those who had already assumed its truth.[17]

Noting that the theme of secularity puts intense pressures on this point of view, he calls for Biblical studies to inform the present social action.[18]

The warning came none too soon. If the new stance of secularity and the concern for the church's mission was to have Biblical foundation, there needed to be more freedom of interpretation. The prophet's word would be heard not only as proclamation to ancient Israel but as condemnation to nations today. Freed from the necessity of fitting Biblical material into a unity, it is possible to reject the cruelty of the early Hebrews as culture-bound and their world view as religiously underdeveloped.

Writing in opposition to Bultmann's skepticism toward finding authentically historical material in the Bible, Pannenberg and a group of other scholars put together the symposium *Revelation as History*. The thesis is that all history is revelatory of God and that one may not limit God's self-disclosure to particular events.[19] This broadens the basis of what might be construed as "holy history." The action of God may be understood in many histories. To Teilhard's affirmation that God was made known long before the time of recorded history and to Whitehead's insight that God is known in every process of creation, the writers assert that God is known in all recorded actions of his people everywhere. This opens the possibility of learning about God from other religions.

The existentialist approach to Biblical interpretation found a focus in the work of two German theologians: Gerhard Ebeling and Ernst Fuchs. These men have said that the Bible speaks of God's saving action only when people understand it to be so in their situation. Although in some objective sense the Bible speaks its own word, this becomes the word of God only when it is perceived to be such by the hearer. The new hermeneutic asks the question, What does God say to me in my existential situation through this word in Scripture? Then Scripture becomes a living word.[20] The dependence on Bultmann is clear. The value of this viewpoint is the insistence that the Bible has words that pertain to human need in various situations. The weakness is that, tied to a specific philosophical viewpoint, it can become dated in the changing theological climate of this time.

The two constructs (the Bible speaking through its own time and the Bible speaking existentially) are strands of long duration in the history of exegesis. An overemphasis on one can lead to a frozen history to which modern people would remain indifferent. Overemphasis on the other can imperil the integrity of the historical record.

Questions regarding Biblical interpretation are at the heart of the teaching task. Without recourse to the Bible, Christians, like Jews, cannot function as a religious community. The Bible forms an essential part of every gathering for worship. Several large Christian groups are developing a common lectionary on a three-year cycle, which affords more diversity than an annual cycle permits. The task of the preacher is to note the interrelationships among the lessons, searching both the historical context and its place in current social and personal contexts. This is a demanding work requiring the courage of conviction and the willingness to stand by an interpretation. Encouraging laity to study the lessons individually and in small groups is another possibility for Biblical study. A post-service discussion of Scripture and sermon is one opportunity. The Word in the Bible has been a wellspring for action; it made Augustine a believer, sent Carey to India, and inspired Christian social movements through many centuries. This power is still available, whether through word of judgment, prescription for renewal, or assurance of pardon.

The language in which the Bible is read today presents problems to some devout hearers. In a time of change, even the Scriptures will be heard in different versions. This is unsettling, for many Christians consider the Elizabethan English of the King James Version or the Rheims-Douay Version to be the equivalent of original tongues. The freedom to move among translations may be appreciated by the young, in so far as they can be interested at all in Biblical material, but their elders are sometimes uncomfortable. Study groups find it helpful to use comparative translations. This gives them some awareness of the seriousness of the task of translation and the difficulty of finding a precise text. The footnotes in modern versions, with their variant translations, add a dimension to the study of Biblical meaning. This is one way of pointing toward diversity and flexibility. Those who have tried to make changes in liturgical forms appreciate the difficulty of gaining acceptance. "Thee" and "thou," never used today in ordinary speech, take on sacred overtones when used in prayer and Scripture, and no amount of rational explanation will convince some devout persons that in the sixteenth century these were the familiar pronouns of the second person singular.

How Will World Religions Speak About God?

The command in Matthew's Gospel is that the gospel be preached throughout the earth and until the end of "the present age." In faithfulness to this command the first generation traveled into the world of Roman religion and culture. Their successors have proclaimed the good news throughout the earth. Today, although located everywhere, Christians are a small minority in the nations of Asia, and almost nonexistent in Islamic countries. They form a growing segment in African countries whose "modernization" process seems to include forsaking the ancient animistic forms of religion. The task of the church is indigenization. Earlier this meant adapting European forms to local customs. Today the fastest-growing Christian groups, particularly in Africa, are those that have broken from their European roots to interpret the faith in forms that link them directly to the experiences of their own people. The early church managed to spread throughout the Roman Empire with benefit of only the most meager relief funds from settled congregations and no full-time "foreign" ministry. It is safe to assume that God does not depend on Western missionaries to keep the gospel alive. Today fraternal workers gather from many places. Only when the people of a nation speak to one another about Christ can the story be heard in accents they will understand.[21]

A new note is arising out of the freedom and varieties of experience available today. There is a willingness to understand the other world religions, to ask what they know about God, and to receive the insights of their spirituality. The first genuine overtures came from the Church of Rome as a result of Vatican Council II. This follows naturally from the Catholic affirmation that God reveals himself in many ways, has not anywhere been left without witness, and that all religions are in some ways reflections of this self-disclosure. Some Protestants, on the other hand, have had an exclusivist view of Biblical revelation that precluded the acceptance of this possibility. When Christians as a minority group have held the faith long enough to feel secure and when their country does not discriminate against them because of their beliefs, they begin to explore the basic understandings they have in common with the religion of their culture. There is Christian-Hindu dialogue in India, Christian-Buddhist dialogue in Japan. The Eastern religions, by nature more accepting of plurality of beliefs, are open to this kind of dialogue. Islam, like the Hebrew and Christian traditions, has held a belief in sole revelation, and these three have found it more difficult in recent centuries to discuss religious faith. This was not true in the late Middle Ages when Arabic culture flourished. The Jews particularly found expression for their abilities in Islamic countries when they were denied freedom within Christendom. Maimonides, one of the great philosophers of that period, was at the court of the king of Egypt for many years.

If the established Christian churches should find such dialogue difficult, they may be led into it by facing the present yearning of the young for a kind of religious experience different from the one in which they were reared. Young people are not indifferent to religion. They have become indifferent to the sameness of familiar forms. Eastern religions promise a fresh approach. In yoga exercises and in transcendental meditation, they seek a centering on that which is uniquely meaningful, shutting out distractions to find clear direction. In Zen Buddhism they seek a guide for living. There is precedent in Christian experience for each. The classical forms of meditation arising within the monastic orders enabled men and women to serve one another and their immediate community in meeting the needs of poverty, illness, disease, and death. The spiritual exercises developed by Ignatius Loyola empowered the Jesuit movement. At a later period, the members of the Society of Friends, "centering in" to receive the action of the Holy Spirit, went out to challenge the injustices in their society, whether it was Elizabeth Fry in England concerned with prison reform or John Woolman in the United States beginning the fight against slavery. Process theologizing brings an openness to explore what Eastern religions have believed about the nature and action of God.

Christians holding unique claims for the person and work of Jesus Christ will have more difficulty coming to an understanding of the role of other religious leaders within God's purposes for his creation. In hotel rooms in Japan, travelers have noted a book entitled *The Teachings of the Lord Buddha*, provided by the Young Buddhist Association. Carefully chosen for apologetic if not evangelistic appeal, these teachings paralleled both the life and the sayings of Jesus. The thoughtful Christian could not help asking whether God was not disclosing himself there.

One cannot speak of world religions without a footnote on the American religion. A series of surveys in the past decade have cataloged its tenets and established the reasons by which people moved from conservative to liberal points of view.[22] Its pervasive folk sayings modify the official theology of the churches. Ask a group of church people their goals for religious education and they will probably reply: teach people how to live, give them belief in God, show them how to follow Jesus, and encourage them to go to church. The American religion is bound up with the dream of the pursuit of happiness, and with the ideal that democracy means liberty and justice for all.[23] The American religion has not changed much in the two centuries since it was first enunciated by men educated in the philosophy of the Enlightenment. It is a good ideal, highly humanistic, and painfully difficult to implement. The Founding Fathers believed that God created the world and that it now runs by remote control (the divine clockmaker). That is a long way from the Biblical view of God with whose demands people struggle, with whose wrath they contend, on whose forgiveness and grace they depend. Yet this American ideal is one element that must be considered in the understanding of God today.

The church teaches about God in a pluralistic world. Many years ago a book was written for children entitled *One God: The Ways We Worship Him.*[24] A decade later *Life* magazine published a series of books and filmstrips on the world's religions. It is time to renew this interest. No place on the earth is more than twenty-four hours away. Interaction among the world's peoples is continuous: in diplomacy, trade, education, and travel. One cannot fully understand the roots of a person's action without some grasp of the religious and philosophical presuppositions.

On the practical level several suggestions come to mind by way of implementing the church's educational approach to other religions. Although the public schools are hesitant to enter the field of religion, some courses and texts on world religions are available at the high-school level as well as on the college level. These could become part of the educational curricula of religious groups. Christians who live abroad should be encouraged to become acclimated to other religions and to share their knowledge when they return home. This is no plea for a pan-religious outlook. It is important to understand both what religions have in common and the distinctiveness of each. Then the reasons for insistence on self-determination by the world's peoples will become clearer and a more sympathetic awareness of the causes of conflict can be gained.

Chapter 7

Being the Church

ROMAN Catholic scholars have been doing the basic constructive work on the doctrine of the church during the past decade. Vatican Council II released new energies of the church into the world. Catholic Christians have always been more conscious than Protestant Christians of being the church. Catholic scholars expressed this consciousness through the documents of Vatican Council II. The first is on the church. Other reports consider the church today, ecumenism, and the Eastern churches. The title of the first chapter of the documents, "The Mystery of the Church," evokes the sense of wonder in this action of God, which human beings can never fully understand or completely control. "The mystery of the holy Church is manifest in her very foundation, for the Lord Jesus inaugurated her by preaching the good news, that is, the coming of God's Kingdom, which, for centuries, had been promised in the Scriptures." [1] There is a profound awareness of the uninterrupted continuity of the people of God from the people of Israel, through the early Christian community and nearly two thousand years of history with the assurance that God will continue the life of his people until the time of fulfillment.

Protestants have tended to find roots in the New Testament church,[2] emphasizing the book of Acts, and have lacked that almost mystical sense of continuity with the people of Israel as a holy people. They find it difficult to encompass the nineteen intervening centuries as being of like character with the first. It is only with this sense of constant chronological movement that one can fully appreciate the emphasis of the Vatican Council II document on the pilgrim church, the sense of union with the heavenly church, and the assurance of hope that comes from being aware of the eschatological nature of the church.

> The final age of the world has already come upon us (cf. 1 Cor. 10:11). The renovation of the world has been irrevocably decreed and in this age is already anticipated in some real way. For even now on this earth the Church is marked with a genuine though imperfect holiness. However, until there is a new heaven and a new earth where justice dwells (cf. 2 Pet. 3:13), the pilgrim Church in her sacraments and institutions, which pertain to this present time, takes on the appearance of this passing world. She herself dwells among creatures who groan and travail in pain until now and await the revelation of the sons of God (cf. Rom. 8:19–22).[3]

Numerous books have been written following the Council, mostly commentaries on and explanations of the documents concerning the church.[4]

The work of Hans Küng is of a different order. He was one of the theological experts in attendance at the Council and his first book in this area, *The Structures of the Church*,[5] was written while the Council was in session and dedicated to Karl Rahner, with whom he has since had some strong differences. The thesis is that the structure of the church is conciliar and he saw this conciliar structure at work in Vatican Council II. He was trying to discover where the authority of the pope as head of the church lay, and he came to the conclusion that the pope's authority was active through the course of a council, but that the pope could not control the calling, carrying on, or concluding of a council.

Küng's next book on the subject is titled simply *The Church,* and is dedicated to Michael Ramsey, archbishop of Canterbury.[6] This is the most thorough and serious study of the church, especially in its Biblical dimensions, that has been made in a long time. Küng begins with historical pictures of the church, looking at each in the light of Jesus' preaching of the Kingdom. The key phrases for the structure of the church are: people of God, creation of the Spirit, the body of Christ. Küng continues by outlining his understanding of the confession of faith in "one holy, catholic, and apostolic church" and concludes with a discussion of ministry and the ministry.

THE PROBLEM OF AUTHORITY

This broad base can hide a basic cause of conflict throughout Christendom today: namely, the problem of authority. It is in this area that Küng and Rahner have come into serious disagreement over the meaning of papal infallibility. The problem is not confined to the Church of Rome, much less to the church in Rome. The doctrine of the priesthood of believers, the office of the laity, the service of the whole people of God, ordination to ministry—these phrases have brought about a shift and some confusion with reference to responsibility and authority. Within any social structure, no one can fulfill responsibility without some kind and degree of power. We are living in a world in which there are great concentrations of power. But at the same time people are pressing for freedom. The church participates in this turmoil. First there is the question of hierarchies that make laws respecting people and situations removed from themselves. This is represented by the struggle against the Roman Curia, the present indifference to the efforts at union represented by the Consultation on Church Union, and the current decisions among Protestant national bodies to break down the overhead staff and disperse them into areas around the country as consultants (a noncoercive word with authority resting in knowledge rather than in office).

In line with this negative response to distant authority is the refusal to grant local monies to national bodies for allocation to services in which the smaller units may or may not participate. Catholic parishes are insisting that parish and diocesan books be opened and that budgets be discussed. Protestant parishes are refusing to raise or to appropriate funds for causes with which they disagree, especially when such allocations are to be decided on a national basis. The result is a decentralization with more power given to those who will give and receive the money. People will no longer observe laws where there is a strong consensus that these are wrong, as evidenced by the massive ignoring by Catholics of the encyclical on contraception.

The recovery of a New Testament perspective on the church has had, for Protestants, the effect of emphasizing the authority of the church as a corporate fellowship, the people of God. No longer is it considered valid to say that everyone is entitled to his own beliefs, or that if you don't like something in this church, start your own. To hold unity within diversity is a painful lesson slowly being learned. This may be one reason why, suddenly realizing how much money and personnel was concentrated in their central headquarters, Protestant parishes of many denominations began to feel manipulated from "above." (There are national gatherings of elected delegates, some of which have legislative power, but these have difficulty enforcing their decisions.)

The recovery of a New Testament perspective has had for Catholics the effect of emphasizing the responsibility of the layman and the place of the parish as the gathering of the people of God, thereby strengthening the "grass roots" movement. Out of this has arisen a new concern for teaching, for being members of parish councils, for reading the lessons at the liturgy, and, most impressively, a situation in which the majority of those attending Sunday Mass will receive Holy

Communion. Their question of authority arises from this kind of lay involvement.

The church has an educational task to explore among people and clergy the relationships between responsibility and power, the derivations of power (from training, work, office, status, God?), and the relationship of the granting and holding of power to the Christian's responsibility before God.

This crisis is bound up with the fact of change, and no one is more threatened by change than church people who cling to the faith that both God and the church are changeless. The authority figure, whether one who sanctions change or one who resists change, is most resented. Current changes are largely in the areas of social action and liturgy. Liturgical changes effect a familiar experience. Encounter with social change involves people in wider social and economic relationships. To help people deal with change is to help them accept authority. This seems to happen more frequently when people can trust the authority figure, when people can trust that this person truly cares about them, will strengthen them when insecure, and will minister to them in their own needs—as well as caring about "outside" needs. It happens when people have full opportunity to voice their feelings, including their anger against the authority figures. The tearing down of the mystique of some authorities, especially the mystique attached to titles, may make it easier for people to deal with the problem. Giving people responsibility and helping them learn how to use responsibility is another way of changing attitudes. The problem threatens the stability of society, and the church needs to stress continuation while encouraging change.

The parish is the basic unit of the Christian community. Its autonomy is increasing within hierarchically oriented structures. In congregational structures, which in recent years have emphasized the national scope, there is a new interest in local structure. The questions being asked in Protestant parishes are nontheological. They arise from studies in interpersonal relationships and from the knowledge of systems analysis. This may be the "Hawthorne effect" at work—that is, any change brings seemingly new vitality. The idea is that a parish should rethink its task and goal, then restructure with task-oriented working groups. This continuous process is designed to incorporate change without blocking it. Both the process and the vocabulary come from computer technology. This is an indication of how the language and action patterns of everyday life affect the structures within which people live. Educational possibilities are built into such a structure. Setting goals is a procedure requiring that participants look at their parish in relation to persons and communities. Defining tasks has theological as well as practical implications, involving trying to understand God's intention for the church and the obligation of the Christian as a member of his Kingdom.

The ministry of the laity is an important element. This subject was first seriously considered in a book by Yves Congar, followed soon by a book by Hendrik Kraemer,[7] each man writing from within his own tradition. Today the understanding of the role of the laity has become part of the conflict and power motif. Next, the discussion of ministry becomes a consideration of the meaning of ordination. Some Christian groups consider all members to be "ministers," and others consider all ministers to be laymen. Churches of the Presbyterian order take seriously the ordination of deacons and ruling elders in addition to the ordination of teaching elders, who administer the Word in preaching and sacrament.

Here is a subject for educational inquiry. Laity need to look at the Biblical background of their role with reference to the present functions of the parish. This could involve intellectual struggle, changing attitudes, and a new willingness to assume tasks. This is not meant to be a counsel of perfection. The hindrances to making people aware and deeply informed lie in the part-time character of their response as well as in the security they feel by remaining unchanged. Radical change, made before people are ready to move toward it, can bring disruption and retrogression.

ECUMENISM

Ecumenism is now a practical reality of the church. Protestants have usually applied the term "ecumenical" to the work of the World Council of Churches, envisioned early in the twentieth century and undertaken in 1937. Recently the number of autonomous church bodies joining the Council has been impressive because of the wide diversity. The membership of Pentecostal groups from Chile and indigenous Christian groups from African countries confirms the purpose of the Council to represent as wide a segment of Christian communions as possible.

Churches in communion with the Church of Rome, however, are so many and so large as to constitute a special situation. The questions may be functional as often as they are theological. Any look at the future has to take seriously the educational task in preparing for the possibility of a World Council of Churches embracing most of Christendom. Hans Küng has made a serious contribution to this study in a section of his book on the church. His discussion of the oneness of the church provides a basis for ecumenical discussion. He sharply outlines the reasons that have been given to justify the separation in the church (He calls these evasions). Insisting that there can be no theological justification for this state of separation, he formulates a few theological principles for "the ecumenical journey of all Churches."

1. *The existing common ecclesial reality must be recognized:* in Christ we are already united—in spite of the conflicting multiplicity of churches.
2. *The desired common ecclesial reality must be found:* the recognition of the unity which already exists in Christ calls us to the search for unity.

3. *The work for unity must start in one's own Church, but with the other churches in mind.*

4. *Truth must not be sacrificed, but rediscovered:* the churches cannot be unified satisfactorily on the basis of indifferentist faith and half-hearted allegiances.

5. *The standard for unity must be the Gospel of Jesus Christ, taken as a whole.*[8]

There is an increasing urgency, not simply about the unity of the church, but about the reunion of the churches. There is today an ecumenical theology. In spite of the fact that some library classifications still regard theological works by Catholic writers as Roman Catholic theology, the reader would find difficulty in making this kind of categorization of most Catholic or Protestant theologians and Biblical scholars. This shared viewpoint is less noted in writings for lay people except in the area of symposia or of books especially designed for ecumenical use.[9] It is still less apparent in materials to be used for the teaching of children, where formation in the tradition is still paramount. However, there is broad interchange in materials used for adolescents. A large number of theological students are studying in ecumenical situations, particularly through the consortia now established in a number of cities in which both Catholic and Protestant theological schools are participants.

There is a broad interaction in the area of worship, particularly in paraliturgical services such as those held at Thanksgiving time. There is some participation in the Eucharist, usually *sub rosa,* and this is the core of the problem of ecumenicity. It will be settled only as those who have authority continue to carry out their discussions on an interconfessional basis. Progress is being made, but the laity become impatient. They do not grant the kind of authority the clergy believe they have. (Whenever "change" is made, one is conscious that it works both ways. Some people resent change; others resent a situation where there is no change.)

Working together will come naturally. There is an interest

in each other's ways, which makes it useful to plan opportunities to visit parishes, observe, participate, and ask questions. Protestant children and young people have been doing this for many years. For adults it is new. Workshops, retreats, and conferences on an ecumenical level are of help. Hospitality is frequently offered by Catholic groups who have the buildings and expertise to do this well. They welcome the possibility of varying the forms of retreat. Renewal movements are attracting both laity and clergy to find deeper insights into the self and into relationships with others.

Religious education in its most specific sense has been one of the areas of closest cooperation. Catholics, faced with their own changing attitudes toward parochial schools, are asking how to accomplish serious religious education for children and young people outside this accepted structure. They need the help of the whole community in solving the question. Many in the Protestant segment do not take the task that seriously and still believe that the Sunday church school will accomplish their ends. With such a disparity of commitment to the goal, progress is slow. One attempt to find a solution is released time, but there are other possible ecumenical forms: in weekday classes, vacation schools, and the shared use of facilities between parochial and community schools. This is an opportunity for Protestants to face the educational task with seriousness. However, trust in the importance of the witness of the volunteer teacher to elicit faith frequently becomes a substitute for teacher training or regular pupil attendance.

THE CHURCH SEPARATE

At a time when Christians as a whole are growing together, specific ethnic groups are deliberately drawing apart.

There is today a renewed sense of what it means to be the black Christian church in America, which unites both the black denominations and blacks within predominantly white denominations. Black caucuses have been established and funds appropriated for their work. A black theology is developing, and there is a resurgence of interest in the specific forms of black preaching and black hymnody, as well as white gospel hymnody of the late nineteenth century. The National Council of Churches has a department designed to encourage developments in religious education for blacks.[10] Denominations that were formerly hampered by lack of funds from moving into more lively curricular formats and more distinctive writing are now able, through shared experience, to make changes as their people desire. Whether black parents want their children to learn from traditional Biblical material, the latest integrated curricula, or black-consciousness-oriented curricula remains to be seen. All three options may be needed.

The Indian Americans are insisting on their right to maintain traditional forms of religion, to accept white American religions, or to modify their Christianity, adapting it to an indigenous form. Their life in the church has until now been maintained by the dominating religious groups, who sought to "do good" for them. Now it is realized how poorly they have been served: little education, desperate social and economic situations leading to deteriorating family life among a people whose basic life-style has been a communal one and who normally would be skilled at sustaining family relationships. They are demanding that their own people be their clergy and judicatory leaders, with autonomy within denominations.

Similar demands are being made by Spanish-speaking Americans, the majority of whom are Roman Catholic. When they arrive as new immigrants in the large cities, they are drawn to small evangelical storefront churches, where they become personally known and befriended. Now the Catholic Church is providing Spanish-speaking nationals to minister to them, expressing concern for the education of their children and the guidance of parents. Families have been reintegrated into parish life, frequently through a shared responsibility in preparing children for their First Communion.

Minority peoples, taking their lives into their own hands for the first time, have a built-in educational procedure. Partly by trial and error, partly by conviction, they will discover what it means to be participants in the whole church by becoming fully themselves as member groups of the universal family. The more complicated educational task lies with enabling those in a majority group to accept this necessity for self-determination. "Doing good" has been the hallmark of the religious person. Works of charity, the keeping of the law, are part of the fabric of the Judeo-Christian tradition. Reorienting people in their understanding of what it means to "do good" is not an easy task. People will need to be taught that helping means standing aside, encouraging others as they reach toward freedom, holding out the helping hand only when asked or when there is the possibility of irretrievable failure. The new kind of helper gives up the comfort of having others dependent upon him and encourages independence. This kind of education involves changing habit patterns (never easy) and encouraging the formation of new ways of perception and action. This is the only way that there can develop acceptable relationships between those now dominant in the churches and those in minority groups.

The problem of the church in the Third World is similar. The missionary impulse has been central in the Christian experience. There is a continuity and outreach from Paul's going to Greece, Irenaeus' converting the people in Gaul, the early churches in India and the fourth-century Christian groups in China. The Protestant movement in Asia is less than two centuries old but it so captured the imagination of people that Kenneth S. Latourette in his history of the expansion of Christianity counts the nineteenth century as the time during which the church showed broader growth than in any preceding century.[11] The dedication of thousands of young adults was poured into this missionary movement. Many of them lie buried far from home. The story is so exciting that there is sadness in contemplating the end. Yet there is rejoicing that the church is becoming indigenized in countries where once it was planted by outsiders. Nationals are leading their own people and ministering to their own congregations. They are developing theologies, liturgies, and catechetical programs, sharing their insights with both their fellow citizens who are non-Christians and with Christians in other lands. The circle is completed when America receives missionaries as fraternal workers from abroad.

The church becomes fully universal when in every country its people can witness and serve as equal members in their society. Church bodies in Rome, Geneva, New York, and other Western cities with some difficulty give up the tenuous power they hold. Hierarchies, like individuals, like to "help." The educational task is so to change the perception of "giving" churches that they will accept all fellow churches with full equality. Enjoying the *Missa Luba* is not enough. (Anyway, it is in Latin.) But having a black bishop at the Council in Rome and an Indian theologian at a conference in Geneva are important. Western Christians have been used to receiving Third World brothers and sisters as grateful beneficiaries of our largess. There should be a joy in welcoming them as fully mature Christians—which they have been for longer than some of us will admit.

The theology of revolution has been heard in the Third World. The writings of both Moltmann and Metz have been of help to Christians in formulating goals for their people. Two books are specifically directed at education in the underdeveloped countries. One of these is *Deschooling Society*, by Ivan Illich, whose ideas are disseminated not only through his lecturing but through discussion groups among those who gather at his conference center in Cuernavaca, Mexico.[12] His thesis is that Western school systems are top-heavy with buildings, administrations, teachers, courses, and years of required attendance and that the Third World is wasting time trying to imitate them. He believes that basic education can be better accomplished by "deschooling society" so that people teach one another and are encouraged to learn at whatever points in life they feel a need of learning. Such learning takes place within the context of a community in order to fit persons for life tasks. Illich's writing has been adding fuel to the fires of dissatisfaction being felt in the United States concerning the effectiveness of the educational system.

Paulo Freire has a more specific theory of education, expressed in the title of his book, *Pedagogy of the Oppressed.*[13] The goal of all peoples, he says, is freedom. This can only come about as they are awakened to the fact that they are being oppressed, so that even the good things done for them are done with intent to keep them "in their place." Therefore they must refuse this kind of bribe and insist, by whatever means necessary, that they be free to make their own decisions in whatever concerns their lives. This is the goal of the revolution: autonomy for each individual. The means are not necessarily "revolutionary" in the destructive sense, for the revolution itself can be constructive. Illich and Freire represent the beginning of a rethinking and rewriting from a point of view that is confident that Third World people are capable of developing their own theory and practice.

WOMEN AND THE CHURCH

Women can no longer be taken for granted. Feminist ferment in society spills over into the church. This can be an uncomfortable form of change, and already it has begun to cause conflict. Church Women United, long noted for being concerned about the needs of other people, have now turned to their own needs. Although as a group church women are conservative, some have become aware that this change might be for the better. Many women today, engaged in outside work, are unable, and sometimes unwilling, to take up the traditional tasks of church women. They notice that women are more often in the kitchen than in the conference room. As long as any are interested in rummage sales, bake sales, and bazaars these things will continue, because they use skills and meet needs. Working women are increasingly removed from church work.

It would be unfair to say that women have had no place in the power structure. In many denominations they have been eligible to serve on the governing body of the parish for many years. They are more likely to do so in small congregations, where manpower is scarce, than in large and wealthy parishes. This suggests to the women that they are deemed capable in small situations but not where large sums of money are handled. This becomes more evident when one looks at how women are employed professionally by the church. As employed persons they rarely reach the top, although recently they have been rushed into high elective and honorary positions. In recent years, there have been fewer women on national and denominational boards than formerly, and even their traditional roles in children's work have been given to men, while no corresponding roles elsewhere have been opened to them. For professional educational work, the local parish has been employing more men, disregarding the skills that women have brought to this area. A man has usually received a higher salary. While women have had fair success entering the field of teaching religion in colleges, they have had less success in entering universities and almost none in entering theological schools.

Ordination is another matter. For many years, this has been available for women in some denominations, but there was never any advancement within the parish ministry. No one seemed to think that a woman's skills and abilities would develop and that she would need the stimulus of a broader field. When the last Christian group finally grants ordination to women it will still be an empty privilege if their talents are not trusted. Catholic women have been bitter about their treatment and they are among the most active in the movement for the liberation of women within the church.[14]

Here again are the basic themes for education today. Women

are deliberately generating conflict in order to effect change in their own behalf. They are insistent on having real power and in achieving self-determination. Traditional Biblical and theological arguments have fallen. Strengthened by the women's liberation movement within society, church women demand action. No one gives up power without a struggle, and Freire's pedagogy falls on willing ears. This will test religious phrases concerning mutual love and forbearance, remembering that women outnumber men in the life of the church. In order for male attitudes to change, women must give trustworthy assurance that they want mutuality and equality and are not seeking to replace one hierarchy with another.

One of the more specific tasks is to rewrite curricular materials in such a way as to change the male and female stereotypes. Another is through broader sharing of working roles in the life of the church. Women will persist in seeking responsibility and power and will refuse to do only traditional work, until a balance is achieved. If women should stay away from the church in protest, the emptiness would be obvious.

Chapter 8

The Church and Its Mission

FOR two decades the church in America feverishly built new buildings, established new congregations in expanding suburbs and increased staffs from the local to the national level. It was exciting to be able to command so much money and to see the visible results of power. Finally this came to an end. There was a plethora of small new congregations and of large unused buildings. A changed view appeared, which said the church must not be totally involved in its institutional life but must be fully involved in the world's work. Social problems had become insistent. There was clamor, publicized through the media, for government intervention in civil rights, poverty, and war. The endless round of parochial activity began to seem insignificant, especially when a younger generation, brought up on this fare, rejected the church as "irrelevant"— the big word of the 1960's. The world outside the church loomed large through the presence of the poor and others who were disaffected.

The writings of Dietrich Bonhoeffer were becoming popular and the message he gave was that Christianity was living in a "world come of age," a "post-Christian civilization." The Western world had not considered itself a Christian culture for centuries, but the church had continued to live under this illusion. Some Americans still talked of being a Christian nation, when really, few people took Christianity seriously, despite a decade of church enrollment and attendance figures that were unprecedentedly high. Secularity was a factor grasped by European churchmen decades before the American churches took it seriously. When they finally did, the position of the church in its culture became more clear. Christians are a minority. The culture lives and acts without reference to God. It has no need of the religious premise in order to accomplish its work. Many Christians can no longer believe that in time all people will hear and receive the gospel.

The religious community could become a ghetto, a place and a people set apart, who keep their weekday life in its own compartment and have a Sunday experience together. Alternatively the Christian community can be the setting through which they become motivated, informed, and empowered to serve God in the ordinary pursuits of life. Archbishop Temple's aphorism became popular: "God did not send his son to save the church but to save the world." The whole creation belongs to God and the societal situation is part of the process of redemption where Christians witness through service.

Whether or not the church is commanded to lose its identity is a different problem. Some quote the saying "He who loses his life shall find it" to indicate that the church should act *incognito* in society—give up its buildings and its money, let its clergy become worker-priests who gather the faithful for their common worship. This does not seem realistic. Interactions between the secular and religious spheres have varied within cultures, but the religious group does not usually decline to be a specific institution within a community, performing certain functions in its behalf. Having a strong identity brings problems such as the temptations of power or the humiliation of powerlessness, but either must be faced. The command to serve the world was given to the church as an identifiable community; to act as if this were not so would be faithlessness to the call.

MISSION

Today the church is caught in social turmoil within nations: revolution, war, and other power struggles. Sometimes the church's role seems to be the prophetic one as God's spokesman. Sometimes the role is hidden, in which case the task of the church is to become a catalyst in order that change might take place. Whenever the church acts with certainty, there will be protest, including conflict within the parish, sometimes so bitter that factions develop, clergy leave, and parishes split. The parish's self-understanding and grasp of its role is not clear enough to develop the kind of unanimity necessary for concerted action. Added to this, the community frequently is hostile toward action by the church, insisting that it should speak only on "spiritual," or obviously religious, matters. References to the bitter condemnations of social evil in Scripture bring no response. There is an image of the church as a refuge from the world and a place of comfort. If this means a place to gain strength for tasks, it is an acceptable image. If it means a place to hide from painful decisions and responsibilities, it is a false image, not true to the Biblical heritage. The conflict generated by these opposing views of the church indicates the resistance felt by many people at a change in a situation that has given them a sense of stability. Members of a congregation have several ways of indicating their power: some will withhold money, others will withdraw from attendance, and some will find a congregation more attuned to their way of thinking. This holds true whether a church has elected to be active in social change or has voted to refrain from involvement in community change. The policies are the same; the groups involved differ.

Another place for action is through the witness of the individual Christian. Such a person, risking opprobrium and sometimes endangering his life while acting as a known member of the Christian community, is presumed to be acting out of religious conviction. These act in the name of Christ without reference to the views of people within the particular parish to which they belong. As individuals they can wield power for change within community, nation, and world. Clergy have more trouble attempting such a personal witness, because they are identified with the religious establishment. This becomes apparent when action in behalf of change is made by people within a hierarchical structure, people who are well known to large numbers both within and outside the church. Alternatively, when these are involved in committing the whole church to actions unpopular with some, the negative response can be felt throughout the country. Support is withdrawn, personnel are cut down, and a crisis of identity develops in which a denomination asks itself what is the role of the national body with reference to the constituency. This can be the beginning of a reassessment.

At the same time, two groups have a general tendency to drop out. One is the young generation. To leave the church and to discover their own religious beliefs has been part of the young generation's search for identity. Today this withdrawal tends to continue beyond adolescence, and young married couples less frequently return to have infants baptized and to have children receive religious education. For them church is vestigial, and they have no need of it. If they are action-minded (idealism is frequently part of their stance), they can accomplish their goals directly within their communities.

The elderly leave the church for different reasons. They resent the fact that sermons rarely bring comfort but are frequently critical, urging them to feel guilty about the past and to be actively engaged in social justice. Obviously, to appeal to one of these is to lose the other. In addition, the elderly are increasingly feeling poor. Remembering days when they were active, they will not put themselves in a position of watching others do what they are no longer able to do.

It has been popular to speak of "the servant church" and to

hold up *diakonia* ("service") as the function of the church for both clergy and laity.[1] To some this has a hollow sound, since clergy have always had a status because of their title and office. But the time for this idea may have passed. Some people within the church feel that they have already been servants for a long time. The black laity have been everyone's servants and the idea of being part of a servant church has an ironic twist. Women have been performing a servant role in churches for generations, long before the term was popular or had any glory attached to it. On the other side of the coin, who wants to be served? People in need of help want the means to help themselves, because that is the only way by which they can increase in strength. They realize that the person who helps gets ego satisfaction from helping and security from realizing that someone is weaker. Just as the person who wants to help is suspect, so is the help offered.

The experiments of the 1960's have largely faded. These were attempts to carry out the conception of the servant church turned toward the needs of the world. The era is represented by several well-known names and a number of well-publicized situations in which the renewal of the life of the church was to be accomplished.[2] No one expected that any single experiment was the whole answer. It was hoped only that in the freedom to meet needs in a flexible way on a local level a new pattern for parish development might appear. These experiments provided an outlet for the Christian concern of many people. They announced to deprived areas and to concerned humanists that the church was aware of this dimension of witness. They encouraged the local parish to develop its own program and structure to meet local needs. This might have been a factor in the changing of denominational structure that has now become apparent, although this was not in the minds of those who developed the experiments, most of which were financed in part by the denominations. They demonstrated possibilities for change and a flexibility to meet local needs.

There are several reasons why these experiments did not continue. One factor operative here is that the church can lose identity in its mission, so that what is going on ceases to be, in a technical sense, church action. Or the members, seeing extinction imminent, withdraw from action in order to preserve identity and the church resumes its previous forms of life. For others the secular work of the church becomes its real work and traditional "church work" seems peripheral. These people leave the church and turn to an *incognito* Christianity. In the heyday of government projects, these were among the first persons employed in developing antipoverty programs. Some experiments were aimed at bringing the nonchurched into the life of the church. These came up against the hard reality of a secular culture—the fact that the church is on the fringes of modern life. If the church wishes to provide service as do other agencies, that is welcome. If any return is expected, this is a futile hope.

While one trend of the church is in the direction of being turned outward, there is a corresponding resurgence of privatized religion. The inspirational preacher gives reassurance to multitudes. The certainties of conservatism continue to serve needs. The sect groups attract people because their belief system is sure and because they bring reassurance to those with little social status. Pentecostal groups fill emotional needs. The very small congregation attracts people who are tired of being cogs in the machine and whose personhood is affirmed in a setting where their names are known and their opinions can carry some weight. Churches seek clergy whose concern is directed toward parish needs. Budgets are structured to avoid paying large amounts to national or area judicatories, which might allocate these for programs where conflict exists. Youth have their own privatized religion, whether a Jesus religion or some form of Eastern experience.

THE CHURCH AT WORSHIP

The wellspring of the church's power lies in worship. Here is where the inner core of the committed gather. Only when everyone forsakes congregational worship can a church be said to have completely disintegrated. (The key word is "forsakes." Some congregations may find times other than Sunday morning more appropriate.)

Worship is the sole exposure that most adults have to the content of the Christian faith.[3] Only at public worship do they listen to Scriptural material and its explication in sermon; only here do they learn the forms and content of prayer. The meaning of the faith is expressed in hymns. The form of worship is the way in which the religious community has expressed itself in relation to God through praise and thanksgiving, petition and intercession. Learning is incidental, but it must not be overlooked.

For some Christian groups, the experience is expressed most importantly through the sermon, which both proclaims Scripture and gives direction for living. For others, the basic liturgy is that of the Eucharist, the Lord's Supper. Here Scripture and preaching are part of a total framework. While the form has remained basically the same through the centuries, the emphasis can vary greatly. For a long time this was for many people a service of communion, stressing the personal response between the Lord and the believer within a framework of repentance and forgiveness and an emphasis on the sacrificial work of Christ. The mood was solemn and the language called to remembrance the upper room and Calvary. Emphasis today is more frequently on the present, with some eschatological overtones, rather than on the past (e.g., on the Lord's Supper, not on the Last Supper); emphasis is more often on the whole congregation rather than the individual, on the banquet rather than the personal reception, and on thanksgiving rather than communion.

The Eucharist has become a feast in which the people of God rejoice in his continuing presence. This is typified by church buildings in which the congregation surrounds the altar. The table of the Lord is literally centered. This action becomes a celebration of ongoing life through the resurrection of Christ.

A sense of wonder is also part of the liturgical mood. Mystery becomes less an apprehension of the awesomeness of God before whom worshipers feel their unworthiness and more an affirmative rejoicing in the power of his love to work wonders even in this distressed world.

The result is a relaxed attitude toward the conduct of worship and participation in worship. In the dress of celebrant and congregation there is an almost studied informality. There are pauses while musicians gather or a reader comes to the chancel, announcements are made at length and members of the congregation are invited to add their own. Spontaneous intercessions become part of the prayer of the church. Vernacular translations of Scripture are more tolerated, contemporary hymns more widely used. The second person singular pronoun form "you" is replacing the earlier familiar form "thou" in prayer.

Nothing has been more unsettling to congregations than this. The one secure hour of life has been on Sunday morning. Here are familiar sights and sounds filled with associations. Clergy have come and gone, but the essential form of the service has remained unchanged. One aspect to which older people especially react is the removal of the penitential feeling; the need for confession and assurance seems important to them. Another aspect is the use of unfamiliar translations of Scripture. The modernizing of the language of prayer seems irreverent. Finally, any transposition of parts of the service causes confusion for them. The young, on the contrary, object to the monotony of fixed form, the solemnity of traditional hymns and archaic language. Some congregations have found a solution in the development of different forms of worship. The two strands work together in helping people accept liturgical change. People need opportunity freely to express their feelings while studying the rationale of change. At the same time, any change needs to be continued for a period of time long enough so that by participating, people become sufficiently accustomed to the new forms to accept their normative use. Multiple services have their place, even though there is the disadvantage of separating the congregation into two parts. A congregation would still be separated if either half refused to attend at all.

The "worldliness of worship," an emphasis that took its place in the literature of worship for a while, arouses the negative reactions of a congregation primarily with regard to preaching. Feeling that they face the world's problems five days a week, some say they need no urging to get into the world. It is even suggested that the clergy are not usually in the world that others are being urged to enter. Schillebeeckx notes that Christian worship is essentially secular.

> Jesus did not give his life in a liturgical solemnity—on the contrary, in an obviously secular conflict, colored though it was by religion, he remained faithful to God and to men and gave his life for his own in a secular combination of circumstances. Calvary was not a Church liturgy, but an hour of human life which Jesus experienced as worship. In it our redemption is to be found.[4]

Schillebeeckx points out that Christian worship was originally worship in the sense of the precept "Whatever you do, do all to the glory of God"; and that for several centuries Christians had no altars, while their communal meal merged with their Eucharistic worship. They lived in immediate expectation of the *eschaton*. So the Christian today must see his whole life as expressing the service of God. The church's liturgy becomes an occasion at which believers gather together these experiences in praise and thanksgiving. This is the completion of secular worship.

Leslie Dewart defines worship as "the rendering of ourselves present to the presence of God, whether in the interior prayer which sends no message to God but receives his presence, or in the public and common ceremonies which visibly, audibly, and sensibly unite us through our collective presence to each other in the presence of the present God."[5]

One expression of worship is in the life-style of the Christian.

CHRISTIAN LIFE-STYLE

The church is in the world most specifically through Chris-- tians whose everyday lives are spent at work in homes, factories, offices, farms, or any other place. While, statistically speaking, people with religious affiliation make up at least 50 percent of the population, the number who take this commitment seriously are a minority. This means that as a group they are on the margin of society in spite of personally being in the middle. Is it futile to hope that their life-style might have some effect on the world in which they live? Wars go on, poverty continues, discrimination is rife, injustice abounds, corruption is endemic in many areas. Those who have a radical commitment to some understanding of the Christian life end up demonstrating this in an individual way. This is why the encouragement of the congregation is so important and why concerted action as a congregation is an addition to and not a substitute for the actions of the individual.

Many young people and some older ones showed a sense of radical commitment in the civil rights movement and in the war protest movement. Inevitably the Christian community will not agree on the points at which intervention becomes witness, but the question of what constitutes justice must be faced. It may be easier to talk about love and to avoid the difficult decisions of justice. Scripture insists that love is shown in works, and God's command to his people is to live righteously. Living as a Christian within any politico-economic system is not easy because an individual decision can affect many people. The action which jeopardizes a job causes hardship to a family. Helping one group of people can hurt another. Questions concerning the use of power arise. One theory is that conflict should be deliberately interjected into a situation as a way of effecting change.[6] Can this be part of the life-style of the Christian?

Christian life-style is equally difficult when seen in the

perspective of individual ethics. The terms "situational" and "contextual" ethics express the questions regarding goals and means.[7] There has been wide agreement that rules of ethics are going to be observed with latitude simply because people do not fit into closely defined boundaries without unnecessary hardship. The theory of situational ethics is that each situation must determine how one acts, for the uniqueness of each situation must be taken into account. The contextualist, more moderately, says that decisions must be made on a broader basis; there is a total context within which specific situations can be evaluated so that one does not have to make ethical decisions at every moment. The Christian community is itself a context for decision-making.

These questions arise today in part because of a shift in sexual standards that began early in the century. Divorce and remarriage is the pattern for many people who wonder what constitutes an adequate basis for a long-term commitment to one spouse. Change has become widespread in an area threatening the basic security of the self, and the Christian life-style should be able to offer resources for enhancing personal relationships. Insofar as standards are hedonistic or self-serving, they threaten a society, for some kind of interpersonal disciplines seem necessary for community life.

Christian life-style today[8] puts less emphasis on rationality and more on emotion, less on restraint and more on action. Openness, warmth, trust, and affection are elements in that style. These grow out of convictions about the love of God toward people and they reflect the total life-experiences of an individual from infancy. The qualities of integrity and fidelity, of courage and endurance, are interpreted by some in this context.

Scientific discoveries have raised ethical questions that pertain to the Christian life-style because they are concerned with life and death itself. Methods of contraception and forms of abortion raise the issue of when human life begins. There are also questions regarding the prolongation of life including organ transplants and the use of machines without which persons with certain diseases could not survive. The mark of civilized people is compassion. Only desperate peoples kill infants and old people, and they usually do this to avert the slow starvation of all. Western culture prizes youth and strength, and has prolonged the length of years beyond that of any previous time. It also avoids the painful and the distorted and tries to hide the unpleasant from view. The Christian life-style derives from commitment to one of whom it was said that "he had no form or comeliness that we should look at him, and no beauty that we should desire him" (Isa. 53:2).

The Christian life-style also stands vis-à-vis a technological culture. This can bring an impersonal quality to life. The people who program the machines are in turn programmed. A threat to selfhood arises from the seeming insignificance of persons.

Presumably technology has brought a surcease from the heavy labor that had been the lot of humankind for so many millennia that the Judaic tradition taught it was punishment for the sins of the first humans (Gen. 3:17–19). Western society is basically leisure- and consumer-oriented. The good life is a rhythm of several work days and several vacation days. A theology of play has developed to interpret this phenomenon to the believer with the message that play is good. God rested after creation. Life is celebration.[9] This seems incongruous with the world constantly embroiled in war, where the increasingly comfortable life of two thirds of earth's people is challenged by the almost insuperable poverty in which others are enmeshed. One is made uncomfortable by a culture that flaunts ease of life and rejoices in freedom from discipline. Life on the pleasure principle, released from a puritan morality and work ethic, brings before the rest of the world a life-style that is both envied and resented. It is no more characteristically a Christian life-style than is the ascetic. The life-style gleaned from the Gospels is one that takes no thought for the morrow, that gives but does not accumulate, that enjoys but shares, that weeps with those who mourn and laughs with those who rejoice. Such a way of life requires forbearance, compassion, discipline, and a sense of justice. There is some encouragement from the secular emphasis on environmental preservation. If earth is again to become fair, then simplicity in the physical arrangements of life must become the life-style of many people. Christians should be able to set the example, since this is at the heart of their tradition.

Teaching the Christian life-style is one of the oldest parts of the educational tradition of the church. The earliest cate-chesis for Baptism included explanations of the creed, the Lord's Prayer, and the Ten Commandments—this last being the "rule" of the Christian life. Matthew's Gospel contains three chapters, known popularly as the Sermon on the Mount, which describe the Christian way of life. These have formed the basis for a common moral code in the Western world. The deliberate repression and even repudiation of the Sermon on the Mount is a development less than a century old. Even people who depart from it like to think of this as a foundation for the moral life. The teaching task changes in a time when there is a revolt against legalism, a flexibility toward what is tolerated as moral or immoral, and a blurring of distinctions between the life of the Christian and life in general.

Members of sect groups deliberately keep themselves apart from the world. Christians who affirm that their witness lies within the full life of the world need to understand clearly what is tolerable within the Christian life-style and what is not. The life of members within the community could be one way of seeing the boundaries. Another is mutual discussion and the strengthening of one another in what they believe to be right and good. The serious understanding of sin, repentance, and forgiveness is another way by which the church defines the life-style of the Christian. There is also the study of the teach-ing passages of the Gospels and how these can be translated into life within a complicated technical culture. Most of all, members of the Christian community must stand by one another when personal understanding of the Christian life-style brings conflict: welcoming new neighbors who are not welcomed by others in the neighborhood, refusing unethical practice even when threatened by the loss of a job, holding to a traditional view that seems absurd to the general culture.

The Christian life-style finds its dynamic in prayer, which is the response of the person to God, based on the faith that the love of God enables one to live as Christ. Many traditional books on prayer do not speak to contemporary Christians, and the traditional kinds of prayers often are not meaningful. Vernacular prayers, expressing thanksgiving and intercession in a realistic appraisal of the life-situation, have been helpful.[10] There could be a rediscovery of the medieval art of meditation, infused with insights from Eastern religions that have practiced this form of interaction with the divine for many centuries. Quiet waiting upon God seems hardly natural to the busy, hurrying, anxious Westerner. Yet people are learning that this accustomed harried life-style is destructive of their health, both physical and emotional. They may change for pragmatic reasons. Christian meditation, however, is not self-hypnosis. Without the reality of committed faith, it is empty. The kind of prayer that is integral to the Christian life-style grows, as does the life itself, from the commitment of the person to God as he is known in Christ. It means living as he lived; dying, and receiving new life, through his life and resurrection. Ways of prayer are learned by practice with others within the Christian community. Changes in life-style are possible through mutual encouragement and practice.

Part III

THE MEDIUM: EDUCATION

Chapter 9

The Teaching-Learning Process

RELIGIOUS education, as the term implies, takes cues from two sources: religion and education. The current religious-theological situation has been sketched. It is important now to examine the second ingredient, education.

The church often has taken cues for the educational process from what is happening in general education. While the goals differ, the learning theory and the methods frequently are similar. Recently there has been evidenced considerable dissatisfaction with the educational past. Some children have not learned basic reading; others, on an intensively cognitive diet, have become disillusioned with education by the time they reach adolescence. There is a striving for change, but as yet no agreement on goals. Parents whose children have been deficient in the basic skills necessary to function in society demand structured ways of developing these capabilities. Others, believing that traditional patterns have become too ingrown to be modified toward improvement, call for a revolution that will bring in completely new forms of education. Buildings are restructured to accommodate large numbers of people in learning centers within one room. New kinds of equipment are being introduced, from teaching machines to cassette recorders and movie cameras. Personnel needs are shifting with the use of team teachers and paraprofessionals. Enriched learning environments are sought. There is a cry for flexibility, whether the phrase be "open classroom" or "deschooling."

THE PEOPLE INVOLVED

Learning theory follows several paths. The developmentalists stress the idea that learning must follow the pattern of the child's development, which can be encouraged but not forced. Erik Erikson has described the stages in psychological development, with detailed emphasis on the preschool child. At each stage, he says, the child may turn toward the next, or, if his experiences have been negative, regress to an earlier stage.[1] The school-age child finds satisfaction in developing skills; the adolescent seeks identity; and the adult seeks fulfillment in work, marriage, and incorporation into community. According to a developmental point of view, it is useless to try to teach until the child is ready to learn; until there is trust, autonomy cannot develop, and until there is a sense of accomplishment, identity will not be achieved. The effect on religious education has been a concern for the human environment offered the learner.

Jean Piaget, a Swiss psychologist, has observed the steps in cognitive development. He records that the young child is in a sensory-motor stage (learning by doing), grows into a concrete operational stage (in which thought processes are concrete), and at about the age of twelve enters an abstract operational stage, beginning to be capable of conceptual thinking. The thesis is illustrated by observations of children in action, and the steps are charted in the child's understanding of time, distance, the view of the world, moral judgment, and so on.[2] The effect on religious education has been a rethinking of the child's ability to grasp Biblical material and theological concepts.[3]

A reaction to an intensely cognitive approach to education is made by Richard C. Jones, who explores the affective side of learning. Watching the reactions of children to documen-

tary films on Eskimo life which were supposed to elicit thinking on how people structure their lives for survival, he con-
cluded that children were so disturbed by the cruelties of life
depicted that they were not functioning cognitively. Only
after they had been encouraged to explore their feelings were
they able to concentrate on cognitive learning.[4] The implications of the emotions for learning have not been seriously dealt
with in religious education.[5] Biblical material could arouse
strong emotions and ambivalent feelings on the part of children: Cain and Abel; Jacob, Esau, and Rebecca; Joseph and
his brothers; the children left by their mothers (Moses, Sam-
uel); David and Goliath; David and Jonathan. Yet these are
usually taught for factual content or theological meaning.
Emotions are involved in artistic appreciation and expression.
Imagination and creativity, basic factors in both the arts and
scientific hypothesizing, are in need of analysis in religious
terms.[6]

A different view of learning is that of operant conditioning,
attached to the name of B. F. Skinner.[7] Skinner says that learning is a simple, observable, mechanical process. Indicate to
the learner what must be done, break down the learning into
simple steps, reward correct responses, and eventually the new
behavior will become "stamped in," that is, learned. Advertis-
ing is based on this thesis, whether the picture-with-slogan
that greets one from magazines, newspapers, and street posters,
or the oft-repeated television commercial. Skinner also warns
that punishment for wrong answers inhibits learning, because
the learner becomes anxious and is less likely to function cor-
rectly. These techniques have been used for dealing with emotional problems, the teaching of retarded children, "discipline"
situations, and the learning of skills and information through
"programmed learning." Programming has been tried in several church school curricula, but in the form of programmed
books rather than machines. The idea has not really taken
hold. Few people are so committed to the theory as to believe
that human beings can be conditioned in every area of life.

The variables are numerous. If the experiences of attending church are good ones, a person will want to join in congregational worship with regularity. If the experiences are negative, church attendance will be avoided. If a class or study group strikes vital interests, those attending will continue to be involved. If it is dull, attendance will drop. If teaching is a satisfying experience, people will volunteer to teach. If it is discouraging, recruitment will become nearly impossible.

Perception has not been a strong note in recent learning theory, but it may enter into the current emphasis on an action–reflection methodology. The theory is that a restructuring of the way a person perceives reality is the first step in changing one's response to a situation, and in modifying attitudes.[8] Sometimes a new way of acting can be a factor in this change. Perception is less frequently changed through cognitive study of a situation. In the major forms of learning and relearning facing the church today, the restructuring of perception is important. It does not often seem rational to accept change, share power, or permit self-determination. Conflict is not usually averted or resolved by rational means (although one hopes there is a component of rationality), but because those involved are able to perceive the situation in a new way.

The teacher sets the environment for learning. The teacher builds a relationship with learners that permits mutual trust and a positive atmosphere in which learning is rewarded by praise, and where mistakes are used as part of the learning process. One noted learning theory, that of Jerome Bruner's, concentrates on the teaching process itself.[9] His basic thesis is that the essential structure of any subject area can be presented in a form simple enough to be grasped by the youngest child, and can be successively enlarged upon as the cognitive powers of the learner develop. He points to the child's curiosity, striving for mastery, and yearning for approval as elements that encourage learning.

One can no longer think of a school situation as consisting only of one teacher and a number of pupils. Team teaching is a productive way of sharing skills, providing attention for smaller groups, and developing a larger number of learning options within a classroom. Resource persons who move from one class to another enrich the teaching process. Paraprofessionals have helped teachers by keeping records and working with individual children.

Parents form an integral part of the learning process, primarily for informal teaching. Their attitudes and actions in family and community relationships indicate their positive interpretation of or indifference toward Christian faith and practice. Simply by their participation in and attitude toward the church they teach. Deliberately planned learning experiences (or lack of these), whether reading, use of television, visits, or travel, are enriching. The meaning of festivals, the significance of birthdays and other life events are taught through family observances. Parents teach a child to pray, introduce the Bible or Biblical stories, use religious music, or celebrate religious festivals.

Another function of parents is only now becoming widely noticeable: their involvement in decision-making for education. Parents in cities are insisting on the privilege suburban parents for a long time have had, of being more involved in the choice of school boards and having boards sensitive to their wishes for education. This has raised the question of the complementary functions of home and school in education, and clear definitions have yet to be made objectively by those concerned. Church education might be different were parents to take an active role in decision-making. They would then have to face decisions about what they believed, what they wanted their children to be taught, how to find qualified teachers, and about the times and settings for religious education.

GOALS

The term "goals" has descended recently from that lofty plane where it described things hoped for. Today, "goals" de-

scribes the possible, while overarching "purposes" and long-
or short-term "objectives" describe what is hoped for. The
term "goals" refers to observable performance and behavior.
This change in viewpoint has resulted from a demand that
children be adequately prepared for higher education and for
jobs. Specific goals can be used to measure the effectiveness
of learning. This is the key to evaluating the quality of education.

Several kinds of goals function in a learning situation: those
of teacher, of learner, and of parents (and community). The
goals of the school reflect the values that a community holds
important. A recent criticism has been that these goals indicated a desire to train people for particular societal roles and
so prevented education for upward mobility. Minority groups
believed their children were being trained to remain in a
servile capacity. Women have noted that, as reflected in reading materials, girls were encouraged in particular activities
that defined their future role and qualities as women. Parental
goals for children, through learning in family settings, can enhance and enrich learning. It was noted that when a popular
children's television program was adopted by middle-class parents for their children, the presumed head start that this was
supposed to give children from less educationally oriented
families disappeared.

Teacher goals are various: to stabilize the position held, to
win promotion, to improve teaching skills, to see learning results. There are also varying pupil goals: to achieve results, to
satisfy curiosity, to please teachers and parents, and to keep
friends. Unless these goals are taken into consideration, the
performance goals of the school will not be met.[10] The adolescent may begin to develop future-oriented goals. Adult education can be structured around felt needs and specific goals.

Thinking about the nature of goals has become a part of religious education. The National Council of Churches has set up
an analytic set of taxonomies to guide in curricular development.[11] The United Presbyterian Church U.S.A. has been the

first to outline behavioral goals at the start of a new curriculum and to use those in the preparation of each course. These goals are described in terms of the development of certain "abilities." [12] Such goals are not directed toward the assimilation of information, but toward the formation of attitudes expressed in habits of action. Conditioning is incorporated as an element in the teaching-learning process.[13]

FLEXIBILITY

The physical environment of learning in the public school is in process of change. Rooms have been enlarged and hallways are used to accommodate learning pictures, writing boards, and groups spilling out from classrooms. Rooms have been built around a central resource center so that teachers and pupils could have easy access to material. The isolation of one teacher and her class has been broken through the introduction of paraprofessionals and team teaching. Older children in nongraded classes help younger children. Individuals move with ease from homeroom into an advanced reading class or into remedial arithmetic. Procedures are flexible, but the goals are specific. There is no pressure for everyone to achieve a goal at the same time or by the same path.

Children of several ages may be in one grade at a particular hour because they all read at the same level, but children of several learning levels may be in the same room at another time because they are involved in the arts, either creatively or for appreciation.

The open classroom is a response to this flexibility. In use in some English schools for more than a decade, it is becoming popular elsewhere. It is based on Piaget's thesis that each child develops at his own pace through each stage of cognitive learning by a process of accommodation (perception modified in terms of new learning) and assimilation (incorporating the new learning). This can most effectively happen, say the educators, if each child can choose his own materials and methods from a number of carefully structured experiences.[14] Thus, each teaching center is an enriched study area for arithmetic, reading skills, writing skills, science, or social studies. Each child spends some time at each center during a day and has an individual conference with the teacher to see where more work is needed. The child's diary and the teacher's observations plus work accomplished are the basic information for the evaluation of progress. The teacher's role is that of guide. Each child learns to become aware of his needs and to take steps to meet his performance goals; in short, he learns to take initiative for education personally. This has been done with large classes of children. It requires a degree of orderliness and respect for authority on the part of the children as well as skill on the teacher's part to give freedom within boundaries.

Other forms of flexibility in education are indicated by such innovations as "schools without walls," which use the resources of a city as learning centers, and street academies, which try to get away from the traditional school environment because it has set up such negative feelings in the learners as to inhibit their learning.[15]

One would expect these innovations to hold promise for church education, where settings vary widely. The church has pioneered in informal educational settings, such as summer camps and conferences, field trips, workshops, and meetings in homes. Yet the classroom model is persistent, and the leader-discussion format is still widespread. However, some adaptation of the open classroom is being used in some parishes. The large assembly hall becomes useful again, but now stripped of the cubbyholes that used to delimit classes. Small classrooms have doors opened, so that each becomes a learning center and pupils move among them. Resources are pooled. Children choose books according to reading ability, a wide age group can watch a filmstrip, and any number can work contiguously while writing stories or making posters. Small groups participate in discussion. Quizzes and games can be used as indicators of learning needs or learning accomplishments. The format is usable whether material is Biblically or experientially oriented. Resource people can be helpful to a large number of learners during a single session. Those who work with adolescents have learned that flexibility is essential and that the farther one departs from the school model the more likely will be some measure of achievement in working with them.

THE ADULT: A SPECIAL GROUP

Adult education has been a concern of American communities since the end of the nineteenth century.[16] That was when education turned from the aristocratic European model to become an aid for the incorporation of immigrants into the culture and for the provision of access to more job opportunities for the unskilled. Language classes and skill training became part of the night school curriculum, later supplemented by basic courses for the completion of requirements for a high school diploma. Courses in crafts and in general culture were added even later.

At a much later time serious forms of adult education were provided by business corporations. Executive training was developed, ranging from several days of sensitivity training to several months in a European setting, learning a language and being oriented to the culture of an overseas assignment. Sometimes staff members are trained to understand company processes with which they do not deal in their specific work. This gives flexibility to managers and helps them to understand the total range of a corporation's life. Conference centers provide an atmosphere in which serious work can sometimes be done apart from the stresses of daily office routine. Serious papers are presented, case studies are discussed, and resource people are questioned.

However, gaps still exist in the adult educational structures. Since people change their work areas in the course of a lifetime, further educational and training opportunities will have to be provided for them. Yet adults frequently find themselves thrown in with young people who do not have the same background of life experience, with the result that both the forms and content of education leave them frustrated and resentful. American education is not yet fully ready to meet adult needs.

Education for retired people frequently becomes superficial. Activities in a senior citizens club can be made a substitute for continued participation in the real work of the world. Distinctions between real work and real play become blurred. While having a place to go to and activity in which to participate are important, many older people sense that what they are offered implies that their performance is unimportant and that the work they do is not really usable.

The models for adult education developed in the community often become models for the church. The pattern for older adults' activity in the community finds a parallel in some church adult groups as well as in "golden age" centers that the churches sometimes sponsor. The pattern for working-age adults in training for skills finds its parallel in the kind of leadership education usually carried on. The pattern for executive education is paralleled in a pale way by upper-level lay leadership training and upper-echelon denominational and interdenominational conferences. There is no parallel for the annual-to-quadrennial judicatory meetings that involve large numbers of laity and clergy (stockholders' meetings, perhaps?). But general-education models give few leads for achieving the goals noted earlier for the religious education of adults. The out-of-town conference, if the group is small, could make possible a complete living and learning environment for brief periods of time. The community group has some potentiality for intensive learning, provided it meets frequently, as for a long-term weekly commitment involving some kind of observation and experience during the intervals between meetings.

Adult learning in the church has long been stereotyped in a leader-discussion format. Catholic educators are now becoming interested in lay study. Having few precedents, they could become innovative. Recent writing and curricular development indicates such a trend.[17]

All aspects of the teaching-learning process have something to say for religious learning, but each must be utilized in terms of a specific goal and a specific group of people.

Chapter 10

The Community and Learning

EDUCATION is a function of the community, which sets the goals and determines the content. In the current American context there is little agreement on the direction the schools should be taking. Criticism has been mostly negative, clearing the air by specifying what is wrong. Recently it has seemed as if there were two voices: one advocating reform to improve the system, another calling for revolution to get rid of the system and begin anew.

RADICAL EDUCATION

The proponents of radical solutions are usually from underdeveloped countries. Ivan Illich insists that it is futile for underdeveloped nations to attempt to imitate Western school systems because of the cost.[1] He says that schooling cannot be equated with education, and that education is better accomplished by having those with skills teach those who need to learn. The government should pay such teachers and should make available to each person a sum of money in educational credits to be used for educational experiences at any time of life. Illich is particularly critical of the fact that a disproportionate amount of money is spent educating (schooling) those between the ages of six and sixteen, before education for life has really begun. (The church does the same in terms of materials, leadership, money, and learning environment.)

Paulo Freire, originally a teacher in Brazil, also wants education to be restructured. In *Pedagogy of the Oppressed* he sets forth the thesis that education for the world's poor people must be of such a nature that through dialogue they recognize their objective situation and are made aware of their dependency. "Generative themes" would relate to their universe and help them begin the practice of freedom. "Limit situations" are the myths and situations set up to keep people "in their place." Perceiving this is a step toward freedom. They are encouraged to reflect on their "situationality" in such a way that they are challenged to act upon it.

Freire says that "word" always includes reflection and action. Verbalism is idle chatter; activism is action for its own sake. He says:

> Action and reflection occur simultaneously. A critical analysis of reality may, however, reveal that a particular form of action is impossible or inappropriate *at the present time.* Those who through reflection perceive the infeasibility or inappropriateness of one or another form of action (which should accordingly be postponed or substituted) cannot thereby be accused of inaction. Critical reflection is also action.[2]

Freire has developed a methodology to accomplish his educative purpose and indeed was successful enough in educating Brazilian peasants for freedom that he found it necessary to leave the country!

Angry books have been written by young men who have tried teaching in the American public school system and found resistance to new ways.[3] Their descriptions of daily life in the classrooms of city schools indicate that education, as they experienced it, is so negative in its total effect on pupils and teachers that it seriously damages the lives of all involved. There was nothing to assist them in their struggle: the buildings were dilapidated, resources including textbooks were minimal, older teachers had evolved methods for survival that were unacceptable to new teachers, the administration had no inner authority, homes and community gave little support. (If this sounds like some Sunday church schools, there might be a parallel—except that one hour a week is more bearable than are twenty-five hours.)

Innovations have been tried that range from therapy schools for handling the hostility of neglected children to experimental forms of education that could engage the intelligence of young people in meaningful learning experiences.[4] These are efforts at reform within the existing system.[5] James E. Coleman, in a research study of high schools, uncovered the massive indifference and boredom there, whether the school seemed educationally acceptable or desperately in need of change.[6]

Faced with continuous deficits, communities seem unlikely to improve the physical facilities of schools now so deteriorated that they are better torn down. Such communities hope that the effects of a lowered birthrate will soon be apparent. A consumer culture that for years rejoiced in a sellers' market provided by successive waves of infants, children, and teenagers, is now content to accept a leveling-off process. In a few years the kindergartens will be smaller, and pressure on the elementary schools will lessen. The junior high students can be returned to the lower school buildings and the high schools can try to serve adolescents. Meanwhile, the teacher so avidly sought just a few years earlier becomes jobless. The schools, instead of rejoicing in small numbers, say they cannot afford certain services because they have so few pupils. Neither child nor teacher wins.

Radical education should be taken seriously by the church, whose gospel speaks of freedom. This would involve a willingness to encourage teachers to free themselves from economic, political, and class boundaries, even if this disturbs the *status quo*. Can Christians accept education for change? Modification is not fully change, but it can be useful in making a situation bearable.

Radical education would make people conscious of selfhood and set them on the road to self-determination, where they would no longer be looking for a helping hand. A gifted teacher among the aborigines in Australia, Sylvia Ashton-Warner, found that if she permitted children to speak the words that held meaning for them—love words, hate words, fear words—then wrote each word on a card and gave it to the child, the children quickly learned how to read, how to use words in sentences, and how to write.[7] Their living experience became vocalized and clarified. This sense of reality in using human experience makes education valid. The learner can see that what is being learned is true to experience. These are the building blocks for new experience and for reflection upon it.

The radical educators are speaking for oppressed peoples and the church needs to listen. The gospel has been preached all over the earth as a word of deliverance. Earlier this was interpreted to mean freedom from illness and freedom from ignorance. It was directed at helping people live within a system, although missionaries have been ordered out of countries because of their involvements in freedom movements. The import of this new form of education is more difficult for Christians to understand. It carries to the ultimate point the affirmation that people should be educated to think and act, directing the learner to challenge the order of society. People are being taught to welcome change and to use conflict (destructively if necessary, constructively if possible) as a way of building a new life.

LEARNING IN THE COMMUNITY

Schools run on money. Property has always been considered the basic form of wealth, so it was natural that schools should be supported from real estate taxes. But this has created imbalance in the quality of schooling because land values vary so widely from place to place. So state aid and federal programs have attempted to redress the balance. This whole concept is currently being rethought.

How money is spent is a responsibility of the local school board. Those who live in suburbs have been used to schools responsible to the community and serving its needs. Known citizens were its members. The administrative officers, especially the superintendent, were chosen by them as representative of what they hoped would be accomplished through the schools. The schools were set up to reinforce community values in the lives of its children and to fit them for the kind of life and work the community deemed good.

This kind of school board has not always been available to cities or to the poor. Money tended to be allocated in such a way that schools in middle-class neighborhoods were favored over those in poverty neighborhoods, although the latter children were more in need of extra help. The mobility of the middle class makes it possible for them to keep moving beyond the city in search of better education for their children. The poor remain. This is a root of the present insistence by the city poor that they should have a voice in the education of their children. Perceiving that real changes in education rarely reached them and that the educational system was becoming less tolerable, they made it clear that they had ambitions for their children and that they believed it was the job of the schools to teach and not to blame families. Out of these demands have come community school boards. People without skills in participating in committee work do not become adept immediately. Time is required to develop cohesion and to learn political maneuvering.

Imagine what would happen if churches took their education boards seriously, inquiring into the goals of Christian education and the means for achieving goals. Suppose the board faced the serious issue of change and conflict as basic material for their educational task. The members would suddenly realize that their work was concerned with adult interrelationships rather than with closely categorized age groups. Suppose they honestly faced the place of education within the power structure of the church, noting the status of volunteer teachers and

of the educational professionals on the staff. They might look
at the minister's own view of the educational task and the expectations of the parish. Such an assessment could be the first
step toward revitalizing the educational work. One could carry
on the same process at area and national levels with enlighten-
ing effect.

There is awareness that the family has a role in education
but there is little real specificity as to what it should be. Concern with television for children has centered around the fact
that this is viewed in the home. If parents can become concerned about their children's activities here, it is reasoned, this
is a first step in helping them to realize their importance in the
educational process. Special television learning programs are
being developed to teach skills, but few are structured for the
purpose of arousing curiosity and giving broader insights into
persons and places. Teachers began to pick up cues from what
children had learned from the programs.[8]

Family living can enrich the learning process because the
time spent there is so much longer than the time spent in
school. This enrichment takes many forms: the essential one
being conversation between parent and child through which
small children pick up basic vocabulary, sentence structure,
and the ability to express ideas freely without the awkward
hesitation which is noticeable where a child is ignored or crit-
icized. The home can offer books, games, puzzles, records,
even home movies and excursions—a broad input of deliberately planned, but informal, educational experience. The
school cannot replace such experience because of the time
factor, but it can teach basic skills and help the child develop
cognitive abilities. Learning also takes place because of the
group setting in the home, where knowledge is gained of how
such a structure works: the interrelationships with peers and
with authority figures, how to deal with ethical situations, and
how to acquire skills of participation in a working group.

Andrew Greeley's study of Catholic parochial schools indicated that the religious teaching in the school, systematic and

continuous as it was, was not nearly so influential a religious factor in the lives of children as was a home in which the faith was taught and practiced.[9] Protestant Sunday church schools, supplying less-professional teaching, are even more dependent upon the practice of religion by the family: in terms of reading, conversation, religious celebrations, and involvement in the life of the parish.

One of the continuing discussions in educational circles is on the responsibility of the schools for character education, or the teaching of moral and spiritual values, sometimes construed as training for citizenship. How does one teach honesty, courage, or ethical living? Who determines what is a moral action? The department of education of the province of Ontario, Canada, made a study of this subject. The province has had the British practice of teaching the content of religion, but it was decided that, in its present form, this teaching was unrelated to the life of the learner. The officials did believe, however, that the school has a responsibility for the moral development of the child and recommended that this kind of instruction be seriously incorporated into the curriculum.[10]

The subject is open to several interpretations. It can be said that character education is not the task of the school, which has a practical work to perform. To say this is not to deny the fact that learning takes place as the members of a class deal with ethical situations that arise as part of classroom living. Or, it might be said that this kind of teaching is an "innoculation" that makes the learner satisfied with the humanistic understanding of the ability to live with courage, honesty, and kindness, and that prevents the religious understanding that God is the source through whom comes the power to live in such ways.[11]

Training in citizenship is a function of the school. The heritage is understood through historical studies, arts, and literature. Citizenship is practiced through the way the life in a school is ordered, particularly in how its administrative structure is democratized and responsive to the needs of all persons involved in the life of the school. The democratic structure is frequently so illusory that adolescents have begun to protest its phoniness as carried out in high school student associations, newspapers, choices in program-making, and judicial procedures. In most colleges, students have won the right to be represented on boards that deal with their concerns.

If the understanding of democracy is so dimly perceived by the educational system, when shall anyone begin to educate a generation for world citizenship? With national interests still narrow, it is easy to have a patronizing view toward other nations. Newspaper and television reports indicate the continuing tensions among nations. Nowhere else is the power struggle more open or more fearful. Christians have been world citizens longer and in a deeper sense than have other people in society. This is probably more true today, when autonomous churches have replaced the older structure of dependent missions. This bond has always made church people knowledgeable about other peoples. It would be unfortunate if now, with no need to publicize missions work in order to gain money or to recruit personnel, this more profound dimension of the oneness of Christians should be ignored. The interaction can now be on an equal level, and those who know Western Christianity can become familiar with the distinctiveness of Asian and African forms of the faith.

INTERACTION BETWEEN SCHOOL AND CHURCH

The first schools set up by colonists in this country were church schools, as, centuries earlier, the formal education of Rome was spread throughout Europe by the religious orders. Slowly, under the impetus of the Constitution, public schools became established. Church people have always had a concern for the development of schools, from elementary grades through college. As members of the community, they have served on school boards. Teaching is, in a real sense, a vocation.

The idea that the parish as such should be concerned with general education is frequently resisted. This is part of the question as to whether the church should take an official stand on an issue—and even as to whether there would be sufficient unanimity within a parish to do so. It raises a question as to whether a governing board in a church has the right to speak for itself without at the same time involving the parish.

Young people are impatient with the church for refusing to take a stand on issues that should evoke compassion and the sense of justice. School issues vary as to their social import, so it would be possible for a parish to begin by backing important issues that have some degree of concurrence among the membership. One suburban parish, through its board of education, went on record to the community's board of education, urging them to proceed with the building of a much-needed high school. This action reinforced the desires of parents, who were anxious that the quality of education be maintained. But a principle was established. The kind of issues that channel more money into ghetto schools, try to correct racial imbalance within schools, or facilitate neighborhoods with mixed economic strata, would founder in many parishes because of divergent feelings among members. Some would raise the question of keeping the church out of politics, or state that the church's function is to deal with "spiritual" matters. This is a new thrust for the consideration of religious education committees who could thereby enlarge their area of concern, become more knowledgeable about general education, and enrich the educational work of the church through new insights.

School and church interact at the point of the teaching of religion during the week. In some countries it is customary for religion to be part of the curriculum, but the plurality of religious groups in the United States made it necessary for the public schools to omit this kind of teaching. The reading of Scripture and prayer survived until recently and there was a generally Protestant ethos in the schools.[12] Some sectors of the religious community continue a persistent effort to bring religious knowledge into the school curriculum, at least on an optional basis. Some schools include such material as units within social studies, where the sociology of religious groups rounds out the picture of cultural life. High schools are establishing courses in Bible and other sacred writings as elective options under either English or social studies. The adolescent desire to ask questions about existence is sometimes answered in these ways. Technical discussions concerning the possibility of objectivity or impartiality continue, but it is notable that the desire to have religion incorporated into curriculum comes mostly from church people.[13]

A parallel drive is to have religion taught by the churches during time released by the schools. This is based on the theory that religion is part of education and provision should be made for it. Here the mandate for impartiality is unnecessary, although there has long been a practice of interdenominational and now ecumenical teaching.[14] This option has seemed attractive as an alternative to Sunday morning classes because of its potential for attracting more professional teaching. The Catholic Church, until now content with parochial schools, faces several alternatives. Shared time will preserve the religious schools and give children the benefit of special subjects taught in the public schools. Turning the parochial schools into a religious education center makes space available for many options in religious education for all ages. Protestants in many sections of the country have not found Sunday church school adequate for many years, and now the weekend mobility of families makes attendance more sporadic. Sunday has traditionally been set aside for church life, but churches are not sure whether secularization is interfering with their traditional work or whether changing life-styles have made it necessary to rethink the forms and time for religious education.

The relationships between public and private schools become a significant part of the pattern of change. Church-sponsored colleges that had once provided a total Christian environment for young people have recently limited the religious dimension of their programs to the religion departments and an active on-campus church life. And now that state colleges and universities have competent religion departments, although the state teachers colleges seldom as yet have such departments, most college-educated adults will have had an opportunity to study courses in religion. This is a new factor in the education of the laity.

Churches have been fairly active in preschool education and concerned about compensatory education. There are many communities in which space is needed for special education classes. Churches could perform a service by offering their unused space to the community for weekday use. The church's involvement in general education has been largely concerned with specifically religious education. If there is any willingness on the part of a parish to become concerned about the well-being of persons in society, this could be expressed through whatever power its members as citizens exert within a given community and through the outreach of the parish in its own exertion of influence and willingness to work for educational goals.

Chapter 11

The How of Teaching

EDUCATIONAL methods are extrapolated from goals. When projected outcomes are established, methods can be formulated. Specifically these will be methods for the learning of material, the analysis of questions, the development of skills, and the formation of attitudes.

A concern of the church's educational ministry today is to modify behavior patterns. Life is changing at a fast pace, and it seems important that people act in consonance with change. But they need to understand why and how this is happening. And they need some degree of self-determination about when they shall change and when authenticity requires them to resist change.

ACTION-REFLECTION

The "action-reflection" method is being used extensively today among adults as an attempt to get beyond the reading-discussion syndrome. The latter was based on the premise that if one understood a situation or viewpoint, he would change his perceptions and actions in accordance with the new understanding. This rational approach led to the rationalizing of non-change. By intellectualizing a problem, some people felt that they had dealt with it adequately, although in actuality they had simply contained it.

By contrast it is presently held that learning can take place when the learner is active within a situation.[1] The whole self is involved—physically and emotionally as well as cognitively. Once tried, a new way of acting becomes less difficult to sustain and less threatening because it is no longer an unknown quantity. If new action results in approval, this is reassuring and reinforcing. The beginning of a new habit pattern may have been established. At that point reflection on the process is essential, for otherwise this would be simply a retraining process, without intellectual or emotional content.

Reflection takes several forms. The experience can be verbalized through discussion with other participants. Emotions are expressed that way. Technical knowledge can bring new information, and the rationale of the experience can be analyzed. Disagreements can be freely expressed, the underlying philosophy of the action exposed, and an opportunity presented to participants to agree with the approach or to reject it. If rejection is not allowed as a real possibility, the action-reflection pattern has been used in order to modify behavior without giving freedom to the participants.

Reflection is not complete unless participants have done appropriate reading to inquire into the background of the experience and the ideas of others in the field. Such material is brought to bear on the total learning process. Films and tapes could also be used as resources.

This pattern was pioneered by groups formed to help people become aware of urban situations. Another form is the long-standing technique of supervised student teaching with the attendant evaluations, or parish field work for theological students. (Such experiences, however, are introductory to a vocation.) Action-reflection requires a controlled, although otherwise real, environment with certain limitations put on the experience. Possibly its most drastic form was that used by a Chicago training group, whose participants were sent into the city's skid row to survive for several days on the initial dollar given them and whatever other ways they could think of to obtain food and lodging.

The basic ingredient is the "plunge" into an alien situation in order to feel what it is like to be alone, deprived of freedom and power. It is immersion into drastic change, and it presents the fearsome possibility of losing one's identity. Only individuals highly motivated toward understanding and change can emerge from such action with positive learning. Others might become so fearful as to build up a kind of hostility that would merely strengthen present belief and practice. At present the method is definitely tied in with teaching about social change. It would need modification in order to be widely useful in helping people deal with the varied forms of change. Moreover, learners who become enthusiastically involved in the action can be resistant to the reflection process. For them the action is the learning.

Action-reflection may become a form of conditioning, but because it contains many variables, it is not a tightly controlled learning situation. It does depend, however, on carefully constructed activity in which people take specified steps, under supervision, and are rewarded by approval and encouragement for successful completion of each step. The reflection period is meant to reinforce action.

This is a possible learning model for some areas of adult church experience. Action learning has been the form for every member involved in a church committee and every devout member who has survived changes in the service of worship. Sometimes, however, such experiences do not incorporate reflection to the extent necessary to ensure success. For example, liturgical change has usually been preceded by information sessions designed to answer questions and to allay anxiety. But the opportunity to reflect after the event is seldom taken seriously, and the reactions frequently have to be made by participants to one another informally. Roman Catholics and Episcopalians have had particular problems in this respect.

For adolescents, action is the mode of living. Impatient with the adult criticism of their way of life, they willingly view intellectualizing as itself a form of acting, even a game. The action-reflection method was used by an elementary school teacher in a widely publicized situation. The teacher told the class one day that all children with blue eyes would have certain restrictions placed upon them. At the end of the session, and the next day, there was common reflection on what had happened to those discriminated against and what happened to the advantaged ones. Since the emotional effects were carried home, parents also became involved in the reflection.

The term "learning by doing" came into popularity with John Dewey and the progressive educators, and was most frequently applied to children's learning. For them, both the action and the intellectual content were important. Involvement was the key to emotional response. The action-reflection pattern has something in common with the earlier project method. It is not, however, the return of a cycle, but rather a spiral where the older form reappears in a new way. Total immersion in the action is new; the emphasis on action in adult learning is new; the placing of reflection after the experience, with only minimal preparation, is different. But the method has yet to prove widely useful in its present form, and whether it can be used with any but a selected group of highly motivated adults in limited areas of experience is still in question.

"The Medium Is the Message"

Second only to immediate experience are those methods through which the learner has vicarious experience. Such experience is less threatening, more under control, and therefore more widely usable.

McLuhan's famous phrase, "The medium is the message," condenses his theory that people learn by immersion in an environment, usually a combination of the visual and the auditory. Today the adolescent is practically wired for sound, walking through the streets with a transistor radio at his ear. Children sit on the floor absorbed in the afternoon's television show. Schools are rapidly developing inclusive resource centers, and it is standard procedure for most public libraries to include record and film collections.

"Multimedia" is the word used to describe resources that employ a combination of the visual and the auditory. Frequently this includes the use of two or more projectors, such as a series of slides running concurrently with a film as a commentary on it. It could mean two sets of slides shown side by side for impact or contrast. Film today moves quickly, and the young viewer is used to grasping the whole through the impact of quick episodes. One thinks of a Gestalt as the pattern emerges from the units, and some documentaries seem less real than fiction. The mechanics have been so simplified that cartridge film is available for a machine that a child can load. So versatile are filmstrip projectors and record players that these have become standard classroom equipment. Excellent films are available from many sources, and television documentaries on film provide basic resource material.

Listening is another popular activity. Easily used cassettes have found a wide market. Keynote addresses by experts are taped and used as discussion starters in small groups. Information-laden tapes are played by busy clergy on automobile cassette players as they drive from calls to meetings. Children receive explanations of a new process and are given directions for recording their answers to questions. The usefulness of tapes is limited only by the imagination of the user.

The use and production of audio-visual materials overlap. Home movie cameras are used by older boys and girls as a way of sharpening observation and recording experience. Cameras are given to children with directions to record their environment in order to reflect upon it. Movies plus tape, or slides plus tape, become resources for original productions. This provides a new way of looking at religious experience, observing the church, interpreting Biblical material or reflecting on life situations. Taped interviews can give a wealth of information for discussion. Film guides are popular ways to introduce group viewing and give leads for later discussion.

On-the-spot television reporting is completely engrossing, although the power of event can be easily dissipated by disengagement. If the shock is too strong, one can always turn off the switch!

Games provide another form of vicarious action. They are as much a part of the life experience of adults as of children, as Huizinga has pointed out in his classic study of the varied forms of games in human existence.[2] Children are taught reading and mathematics skills through games. Adults have particularly enjoyed games of chance (which, carried to the extreme, become forms of gambling and which can then become a response to emotional problems). Some years ago psychological parlor games became popular. Then it was discovered that games could be used to make people aware of social issues. Such games have now proliferated. Usually simple in form, they may be played with board, dice, and cards. Teaching comes through the interaction of the players and their quick responses to the situation. Later reflection on the plays and results clarifies understanding. Devising games has become a business and a pastime.[3] Games can be used for information. For example, a board game could simulate the Exodus events. Games deal with the results of intervening variables (move ahead, go back, pick up another card). The cards can even be stacked against a player—a vivid way momentarily to share in the life of the underdog!

Complicated games divide players into groups and subgroups. It is possible to simulate a situation in which the players will spend hours working out conflicts, playing off power, and striving to effect the change they believe to be important. Sometimes such games can come so close to life as to evoke the same explosive responses that come in action-reflection.

Resources are so varied today that no one could encompass all the possibilities for curriculum development. The resources are expensive but reusable, and in time a solid block of materials can be built up and used among broad age groups. In the early 1960's a group established by Jerome Bruner began

new curricula for schools, based on the idea of bringing information to children in many forms. Each unit was complete,
whether experiments for science or movies for social studies, so
that any school could have enriched curricular units.[4] Today
that idea has been taken up by denominational publishers and
multimedia boxes abound. Each customarily will include
charts and pictures, filmstrips and records. Some include books
and whatever work sheets will be needed by the class. These
are a way of trying to circumvent the habit of the volunteer
teacher of preplanning so late that it is impossible to find the
suggested resources. The idea may seem extravagantly expensive, but the time for it has probably come. The resource
box will not be fully usable until it is disassembled and its
contents made available to the whole school.

THE ARTS

Another way by which people can participate vicariously
is through the arts. In art the viewer identifies with people
and with situations. Of course, it is necessary to spend time
with art in order to know and feel what it is saying.

Abstract forms of art have been translated into posters,
which are becoming popular in education. Some shout out celebration; others reflect the somberness of loneliness. Some ar-
tists, not content to let the colors or the symbols speak, have
lettered slogans. Less moralistic than those of an earlier day,
they are still attempts to reinforce the pictures. The cartoon is
a pictorial form in which the viewer makes quick identification,
an important aspect being the satirical quality in the situation
or the words. The cartoon brings a resigned word to bear on
whatever the current conflict may be, and in laughing half-
heartedly one sees an event differently.

Music is as all-encompassing as film, in its own way. At the
cinema, one is overwhelmed by size and enveloped in sight.
In amplified rock music, one is also overwhelmed—by sound
—and enveloped in its vibrations. The expansions of a sym-

phony and the full sound of an organ can be brought into any room through the use of high fidelity and amplification. One does not so much hear music as feel it. The words change, and each year has its distinctive theme. Sometimes it is a cry for justice; again, the complaint of loneliness; at another time, the joys of love; or, again, the pathos of parting. The music varies from sweet to bitter; from country and folk to rock and jazz. Many are the sounds of popular music. Many, too, are the sounds of composers' music, for the electronic age has brought in new cacophonies, sometimes imitative of baroque, sometimes as new as the combinations of metal used in the composing. Music liberates, as young people would say. It gives voice to freedom even while it comments on the social scene.

Someday the sights and sounds of a new age will find their way into the church. Architecture has combined the abstract in vivid panes of colored glass, strange to those who thought of stained glass in hues of blue and red alone. The music continues to be as close to the sixteenth century as modern technology can make it. Only occasionally are wind and stringed instruments, brass and percussion (known in Biblical times) admitted. The young would like this, for fixed arrangements disconcert them. But change is difficult for the grass-roots church. The familiar brings such security!

A primary way of having vicarious experience has been through the theater. In the interplay of human situations and emotions the members of the audience see themselves as participants. Theater explores the depths of human experience. Story similarly portrays life, and story theater (or readers' theater) happily translates fiction to the stage. This is actually the ancient way of transmitting history and culture; dance, drama, ritual, and ceremony involve everyone.

Such vicarious action may not in itself change attitudes or alter perception. Yet it permits the participant to look at alternative actions empathetically, inviting emotional response.

METHODS AND GOALS

To single out methods currently popular is not to discount those that have demonstrated their continued usefulness. The priorities in the church's teaching task have lifted some teaching methods into prominence. Change is an action, whether one avoids it or enjoys it. Power is a use of action. Self-determination eventually requires action both by those seeking a new life and by those affected by a changed relationship. Both the threats and the benefits of these actions can be tried and assessed through increasing involvement. Skill lies in choosing methods that engage learners within a supportive environment. From pictures to film, from story to drama, from discussion to role-playing, from games to events, people get the "feel" of the kind of situation in which they must live.

Nor does the presentation of action methods discount the place of rationality in learning. This, too, is an element in the acceptance of change. It frequently happens that only after change has taken place can those affected become calm enough to look at the situation rationally. Then explanation, to oneself and in a group, can trace the causes, the processes, and the results of the total learning experience.

The leader is an important intermediary, whether professional or volunteer, teacher or committee chairman. The awareness of this fact has caused the present upsurge in new leadership training resources among a number of denominational and other publishers, as well as increased opportunities for participation in a variety of training situations. It is essential that clergy leadership be aware of their own educational task, for, in the last analysis, responsibility rests with those who have power.

Chapter 12

A Forecast for the Church's Teaching Ministry

PLANNING has its own vocabulary. One word is the concept of "models." The model may be drawn abstractly, as in a mathematical model, or it may be concrete, as in the model of a building. In either case the value of the model is that it becomes a small-scale objectification of what is planned. It can be modified in any direction; it can be scrapped if necessary and a new model begun. The model has something in common with the scenario, which is a narrative description of the action to be developed. The background for this term is the writing for film. The script fills in what the scenario outlines. The scenario provides a word picture based on assumptions regarding trends of the future. A projection is a look into the future. Such activity is based on the theory that by thinking ahead one can take appropriate steps to bring about a specific form of future, thereby exercising some control over its shape.

MODELS AND THE CHURCH'S TEACHING

The model, says Karl W. Deutsch, serves four purposes. It has an organizing function whereby a meaningful pattern may be perceived. It is a heuristic device through which new facts and methods may be discovered. It is predictive and it can be used for measurement. An adequate model will be simple and realistic and will suggest new lines of investigation.[1]

Cybernetics provides the general modular framework for much thinking today. Its roots are in neuropsychological knowledge, psychology (especially Gestalt and operant conditioning), mathematics, and electrical engineering. This provides a basis for systems analysis with its links to simulation game theory. The elaborate "games" played out in the Pentagon or in the "think tanks" (those groups whose function is to seek solutions for future problems) are the most elaborate application of game theory, but children playing indoor or outdoor games are also developing strategies in order to reach goals.

Not surprisingly, the church has seized this possible method for facing the future.[2] The "model" for religious education has long been the school, rather narrowly conceived as a classroom experience, age-graded, with a teacher as authority figure who has knowledge, skill, and understanding. But this model is breaking down. With the criticism being leveled at general education, the church's educational security has vanished. Its educational outlook faces drastic change with resultant conflict. The usual alternatives are to withdraw—that is, to modify, hoping thus to "improve" the existent structures—or to accept this as a period of uncertainty when various models will be tried. The Sunday morning church school has been a standard form of the model for many years. Signs of the present disintegration might have been noted in the modifications that have been tried for almost a century for curricula, age-grading, classroom methods, teacher training, children's worship, youth groups, and adult education.

There are other possible models. The family is one, despite its own internal changes. The family as model suggests several educational possibilities: intergenerational learning, informal relationships, flexibility of setting—indoor or outdoor—and a variety of spontaneous activities. Although not all families are able to be this kind of learning environment, this does not negate the fact that every child is learning something from the family situation. Family learning has specific as well as long-range goals. Much of the learning is immediately evaluated, approved, or corrected. This is the basic learning environment until a child is about six years old. It has been suggested that religious education through the age of six or seven might best be carried on in small groups in homes and that groups of families structure occasions for religious learning in homes or in an informal church setting. (The equivalent school model is that of the private boarding school, which attempts to combine home and school with somewhat uneasy compromises, but with the emphasis upon being a school.)

Another model is that of the playground. Piaget's research into children's games gives specific insight as to how children make and enforce the rules.[3] Adults have their equivalent "playgrounds," sometimes sex-differentiated: coffee klatch, sewing group, hunting or fishing party, golf course, neighborhood bar. There is also family camping that combines family and playground activity. The strength of the playground model lies in a situation where peers learn and teach each other by developing structures, accomplishing goals, and engaging in reciprocally helpful relationships. Informal groups such as Scouts, service clubs, and specific interest groups are similar examples.

The world of work is another model. People are screened before acceptance, trained in skills, moved from one responsibility to another, and constantly retrained in order to improve skills. There are payments and promotions. The working world has an elaborate hierarchy of command including two classifications of workers: management and labor, the latter having their own organizational structure in the union. The company is an economic and a political structure. The goals are specific; the skills are carefully developed. For some the structure encourages creativity; for others it insists on uniformity.

There are other possible models. Community government is carried on by a group of persons who learn of needs, do research, make reports, come to decisions, and are concerned with specific areas as well as a total context. Professional groups in the arts, such as drama or ballet companies, musical ensembles or orchestras, are learning and working communities in which both new and experienced members learn individually and together, both to perfect individual skills and to enhance the work of the whole entity.

The church, by choosing a formal learning model, has thereby restricted its teaching possibilities. It must now devise particular models in consonance with its own needs.

SETTING THE GOALS

The church's educational work is set in a technological society. Its people feel at home in a setting where life is governed by complex machinery. They take the instantaneous for granted: communication, light, heat, or transportation. Electricity makes tasks easy and comfortable. Modern man lives by the clock. When someone asks how far one place is from another, the answer is given in time, not in distance. Even recreation is pressured.[4] And numbers of people have fled from highly organized settings to search for a simpler life-style.

Science is the groundwork of this technology, with its telescopes and microscopes, atom smashers and satellites. This is the world of which Johannes Metz writes:

> The secularity of the world, as it has emerged in the modern process of secularization and as we see it today in a globally heightened form, has fundamentally, though not in its individual historical forms, arisen not against Christianity but through it. It is originally a Christian event and hence testifies in our world situation to the power of the "hour of Christ" at work in history.[5]

He describes how this has happened. Out of a church-dominated and church-developed culture arose the separate state; out of theology as a science developed the modern sciences; out of the Biblical context arose the objectivization of nature and the dethroning of magic. These steps were slow and painful. Metz's point is that secularity is a positive force made possible by the nature of the Christian faith. This is the kind of world in which Christianity has flourished. He refuses to sanction either withdrawal from the world or loss of identity in the world. Interaction is the mark of the Christian community. As Paul writes to the Corinthians, "For all things are yours, whether . . . the world or life or death or the present or the future, all are yours; and you are Christ's; and Christ is God's" (I Cor. 3:21–23). The same affirmation can be heard in the advice that Christians are to be in the world but not of the world. The quest for a world-affirming Christianity is a primary task today.

This setting has caused tensions for Christians. That which is necessary for the resolution and positive use of the situation sets the goals for the church's education. The use of the term "goal" is deliberate. The overarching purpose of the educational ministry, as part of the whole ministry of Christians, does not change. This is to proclaim the good news that God has shown his love to the world through the person (life, death, and resurrection) of Jesus; that he comes to bring salvation to all people; and that he will, in his time, judge and fulfill his promises. Redemption has different emphases. To people who feel alienated and alone, redemption comes when God enables them to be free to accept and return love. When people feel overwhelmed by the guilt of sin, redemption means the assurance of pardon and restoration. Today redemption needs interpretation to people who feel enveloped by change, power, conflict, and the perplexities of self-determination.

The purpose of the proclamation of the good news is fulfilled through expressed goals. A goal, by this definition, is more specific than a purpose, to some degree attainable and measurable. Goals are functional or behavioral. Earlier reference was made to the taxonomies developed by the Division of Christian Education of the National Council of Churches and to a denominational emphasis on functional goals. This approach has been made explicit by James Michael Lee, who develops a social science approach to religious education. He views the task as instructional with a goal of observable behavioral change.[6]

Seen within this kind of framework, some of the goals arising out of the needs faced by Christians today might be:

1. That people learn to accept change as being part of the Christian experience.

2. That people learn how to use human power beneficently as having the possibility of participation in God's power.

3. That people understand, theologically, the reasons for conflict and learn how to express, live with, and use conflict in positive ways.

4. That people view the drive toward self-determination as a working out of God's concern for the fulfillment of each person created and redeemed by him.

These are not the only tasks of the church's educational ministry but are some of the more compelling ones for the present and the near future.

Learning goes from an observable point "where the learner is" toward a goal. The point of beginning can be ascertained in terms of speech and behavior as indicators of attitudes held. Learners are participants in goal-setting. But to attempt to set goals for people and to lead them toward these goals is manipulative and may be resisted. It ignores the impetus that comes from the learner when motivation is part of the drive.[7]

PROCEEDING TO THE TASK

Information-gathering of several kinds clarifies the starting point. This may consist of responses to questionnaires, opinions from a discussion group, results of interviews, the observed attitudes and actions within church and community on an issue, a request from some people that a study be made, an immediate situation requiring attention. From these kinds of questions, the problem can be described.

The next consideration is to probe the resources available for dealing with an issue. For example, a congregation finds itself in the midst of a changing neighborhood. Changing neighborhoods have been a source of conflict for churches, whether this means low-income families moving into an upper-income community or city families moving into a rural village. Some congregations refuse to make any gesture of welcome and will not consider any modification of structure or program to accommodate a changed situation. One resource available to help such congregations might be simulating situations in which established residents take the role of newcomer and recall feelings in which almost anyone was once strange—first day at school, first day at work, beginning of marriage, arrival of the first child, moving into a new community, or being a hospital patient. Another is studying the Biblical understanding of the treatment of the stranger, the relationships of all people to God, and the meaning of participation in the Christian community. Information about the experiences of congregations that have met a similar situation constructively will be helpful. An interchange of visits to share insights would be helpful. Films could involve viewers in similar situations, and filmstrips could give background material. Printed resources are also available. It is important to work beyond feelings and to objectify them in order that the basic factors at work in the conflict can be seen and dealt with.

Such a congregation, faced with a changing neighborhood, would accumulate sufficient background to look at the alternatives and their consequences. For example, if the congregation decided to remain unchanged, the consequence would be two distinct groups of families, the established residents and the newcomers, living side by side in the community, and a new congregation might be started. The two groups of families, as well as the (now two) congregations to which they belong, might ignore, resent, or cooperate with each other. The advantage for the present congregation would be that it could continue its style of existence; the disadvantage would be the possibility of declining growth and of continued disagreement within the membership. On the other hand, if they decided to be open to the modifications that newcomers could bring, there might be two groups within the church, either assimilated or working in parallel groups, as sometimes happens within mergers or federations. There would be more people, more leadership, and more viewpoints—and these could enrich the life of the parish. Diversity brings problems and advantages.

This is the point of decision. Whatever the choice, change occurs and with it the possibility of friction. The strategy for action would need to include support and encouragement for those who are hesitant in moving toward the goal. The work of change must continue beyond the immediate goal, that of welcoming newcomers, if these are to continue in the life of the church instead of dropping out. The possibility that, in any event, some people will withdraw—both old-timers and newcomers—must be recognized. The consequences of remaining unchanged would be parallel. An essential element is that both positive and negative responses be sympathetically received so that further changes can proceed on the basis of such information.

There comes a point at which those involved in such a learning situation will need to look at it from an evaluative perspective to measure the progress, if any, made toward the goal. The following are possible criteria under the four goal headings outlined earlier.

1. *Accepting change as part of the Christian experience.* A person or group may either actively resist, passively resist, passively accept, indifferently accept, see positive possibilities in, enjoy, or work for specific changes in, a given situation. For example, the morning service is noticeably revised. Some worshipers change membership to another parish; others attend infrequently, attend with minimum participation, accept some portions while resisting others, get used to the new form, enjoy the change, or assist others in accepting the change. For those at one end of the "scale," corporate worship is an unchanging experience; for others, the specific forms of change are less important than the total experience.

2. *Learning how to use human power beneficently as having*

the possibility of participation in God's power. A person or group may (1) actively resist becoming involved in a situation that requires the use of power—to the point that negative results occur to the self and/or to others; (2) passively resist by withdrawal, become submissive, accept the situation indifferently, accept without making the most use of the power structure, although one sees a positive potential in it; (3) work positively within a power structure, utilize power and accept relationship to others in power roles, gain skills in using power and working within power structures for beneficent ends. (These steps are parallel, whether referring to a person offered power or to one with a minor role in the power structure.) For example, a member of a church council (1) may resist every suggestion made in the council; (2) may be passively resigned (rarely speak) or be a noncontributing member (rarely attend); or (3) may go along with those in power when agreeing with the goals, take a share of responsibility in order to further the enterprise, perceive the reality of power and seek actively, in the work of the council, to employ these skills in the use of power. Power is also used negatively by those who wield it for narrow ego-satisfactions or to dominate a situation toward destructive ends. The understanding of vocation that a council member may have can sensitize, creating an awareness of this group as a potential channel through which the power of God works beneficently in church, community, and world.

3. *Understanding theologically the reasons for conflict and learning how to live with it and use it in positive ways.* A person or group may strike out haphazardly, enter the conflict in anger, withdraw with apprehension, have some notion of pacifying, be involved in a struggle to preserve personal ego strength or power, or indicate agreement with those seeking a solution by giving moral support or by working toward the expressed goals. For example, a parish has been asked if part of the building may be used to house a day nursery for children whose mothers work. Some think this is an important

community service; others object because of potential damage to the building, because of the kinds of people who would be using the building, or on the principle that mothers should stay home. Responses might include the following: to take no part in the discussion, to withdraw money or membership, to withdraw but promise to return in response to the desired decision, to try to work out a compromise, to encourage one side or the other but offer no concrete solution, to work for a positive solution both to the need and the conflict (which may or may not involve use of the building), and realistically to assess the losses and gains in any decision and the degree of possible realization of goals. These are steps entered into by any person or group in decision-making. The added dimension for the church is the realization that one can only worship and serve God while reconciled to other persons. As stated earlier, this means, not repressing conflict, but using it positively.

4. *Viewing the drive toward self-determination as a working out of God's concern for the fulfillment of each person created and redeemed by him.* A person or group may oppose this ("I know what is best for you"), may be hurt that one's help is not wanted, try other ways of having the offer of help accepted, take the attitude that the other person or group is not worthy of help, withdraw and try to feel indifferent, accept the idea but hover anxiously on the sidelines, learn how to treat the other as an equal as regards ability to determine a life-style. For example, the adolescents in a parish want to determine their own structures for study, worship, and other activities. The response of the adults might be to insist that they understand best, to be in constant conflict, to leave the adolescents to their own devices, to work out a compromise whereby sometimes one wins and sometimes the other, to let the adolescents work out their own plans but to be available to strengthen or help when asked. This involves a recognition that God is working out his purposes for each person and that those who stand nearby may or may not be useful at particular points.

It should be emphasized that these are not steps toward perfection but descriptions of behavioral response to goal-oriented situations. The goal is partially fulfilled at whatever level a particular person or congregation is able to achieve. Some movement toward a positive acceptance of each goal would be a realistic achievement, but the degree of fulfillment will depend to some extent on the personal history of each person or group and upon individual abilities to deal with issues. However, this does not release teachers and leaders from their task in the development of skills and understanding that will make possible an increasing degree of learning.

TEACHING IN A CHANGING SITUATION

Religious education translates the theology of the church through the needs impinging upon people in their life situations in such a way as to help them to live affirmatively, strengthened by their faith.

The present situation is that of a technological culture, in which scientific achievements have brought both the possibility of freer options in life-styles and the apprehension of destruction, thereby creating an ambivalent attitude. Each segment of the population—whether grouped by age, sex, race, or national origin—has particular needs and grievances. The theological understanding of the church is not helpful, for theology points toward search, diversity, and free-ranging options. Educational theory and practice is no help, for education is under criticism throughout the world, existing in a time of transition. But this can be good. The old school-model is gone: there is freedom to look at the church's education in new ways. Elements from family learning, community action, and the practice of voluntary groups suggest elements for a new educational pattern involving all ages.

The need of people to live with change, understand power, resolve conflict, and affirm the self is met by the church's understanding that God is involved in the re-creation of his world until its final redemption promised through the resurrection of Christ. Because renewal and change are part of God's order, it is possible for humans to incorporate these into their life-styles. The Biblical imagery of a nomadic and a pilgrim people, called to go wherever God sends them, moving toward a goal that will be fulfilled in God's time, expresses this kind of willing expectancy and freedom from dependence on the known and familiar order of life.

In Christian understanding, the Holy Spirit is redeeming and creative power. To understand and to use power (for those whose lives are directed by a relationship to God and his purposes) is to be responsive to the redemptive purposes of God affirmed in Jesus Christ.

The church is meant to be the kind of community in which selfhood is affirmed and security is given through the assurance of God's continuing love abiding with his people and in his world. To understand each person as named by God is to recognize the uniqueness of each and the vocation of every person to fulfill that which he envisions as God's purposes for life. In this kind of environment, change can be evaluated and used for the strengthening of persons and their community. Conflict can be utilized as a positive process engaged in with mutual understanding, a process that does not destroy but rather re-creates. The pain involved in such a process can be sustained by the corporate worship of the church and the determination to be encouraging to one another. Opportunities to speak, listen, and act in this kind of setting help to develop new insights.

Not every change will turn out to be the best decision. Some efforts at self-determination will fail. Conflict will sometimes engender bitterness. Power always has a destructive potential. God has not promised that the church will always be perfect or always "succeed," but only that insofar as it seeks his Kingdom and his righteousness he will sustain it.

These are some of the elements in a Christian life-style. These help Christians face and act upon the difficult ethical

issues raised in any era. So the whole church seeks to fulfill its
calling and to be faithful to its role in the reconciling work of
Christ. The future is unpredictable, and whatever the planning, the human community still lives by hope. For those in
the Biblical tradition, hope is affirmed through the promise of
the continuing power of God working for good through all
things.

Notes

Chapter 1. CULTURE AS ENVIRONMENT

1. Books are becoming numerous in this area. A sampling would include Herman Kahn and Anthony J. Wiener, *The Year 2000: A Framework for Speculation on the Next Thirty-three Years* (The Macmillan Company, 1967); Daniel Bell (ed.), *Toward the Year 2000: Work in Progress* (Houghton Mifflin Company, 1968); Andrew M. Greeley, *Religion in the Year 2000* (Sheed & Ward, Inc., 1969); Lyle E. Schaller, *The Impact of the Future* (Abingdon Press, 1969); Edward W. Uthe (ed.), *Significant Issues for the 1970's* (Fortress Press, 1969), from the task group for long-range planning, Lutheran Church in America.

2. Alvin Toffler, *Future Shock* (Random House, Inc., 1970), p. 326.

3. Robert J. Lifton, *History and Human Survival* (Random House, Inc., 1969).

4. Charles A. Reich, *The Greening of America* (Random House, Inc., 1970).

5. The classical study on this subject is Johan Huizinga, *Homo Ludens: A Study of the Play-Element in Culture* (The Beacon Press, Inc., 1955). A more recent book reflecting theologically on the subject is Hugo Rahner, *Man at Play* (Herder & Herder, Inc., 1967). David L. Miller's *Gods and Games: Toward a Theology of Play* (The World Publishing Company,

1969) is a summary of game theory in anthropology, psychology, literature, philosophy, mathematics, and other areas.

6. In June, 1971, at the first Springhill Conference, held at Belmont, Vermont, a group of religious educators from national and area denominational offices, the National Council of Churches, and theological schools and parishes discussed this situation with the following conclusions for the future: that more flexible portfolios will be needed for educators (being a resource expert rather than an age group specialist, for example); that varieties of educational experiences will be tried in churches; that curricular materials will move toward becoming resources; that there will be a continuing emphasis on including the whole Christian community within church education.

7. Basic studies in this area have been made by Karl W. Deutsch, one of whose influential books is *The Nerves of Government: Models of Political Communication and Control* (The Free Press of Glencoe, Inc., 1963).

8. *Spectrum*, a periodical edited by Harold M. Martin and published by the Department of Educational Development, Division of Christian Education of the National Council of Churches, New York, N.Y., read by laity and professionals, included an eight-page special report listing human relations training conferences under two headings: (1) Personal development: communication, conflict, congregational dynamics, human relations, married couples, personal growth, small-group processes; (2) Professional development: community development, consulting skills, creative risk, educational design, skill leadership, organizational development, training of trainers. (May and June, 1971, pp. 27–34.)

9. See Konrad Z. Lorenz, *On Aggression* (Harcourt, Brace & World, Inc., 1966), for a fuller treatment of the subject.

10. Frantz Fanon, *The Wretched of the Earth* (Grove Press, Inc., 1965), describes the steps in decolonization from the standpoint of people going through the process toward national independence.

11. Among the books beginning to appear might be noted Dee Alexander Brown, *Bury My Heart at Wounded Knee: An Indian History of the American West* (Holt, Rinehart & Win-

ston, Inc., 1971), which, through excerpts from the American Indian's own documentary history, tells the poignant story of the gradual containment of the Indian peoples.

12. J. Stanley Glen writes of a "relational hermeneutic" in *The Recovery of the Teaching Ministry* (The Westminster Press, 1967).

13. See Randolph Crump Miller, *Living with Anxiety* (Pilgrim Press, 1971).

14. Paulo Freire, *Pedagogy of the Oppressed* (Herder & Herder, Inc., 1970).

15. The church as environment for Christian education is discussed by C. Ellis Nelson in *Where Faith Begins* (John Knox Press, 1967).

16. Editorial, *The New York Times*, Jan. 9, 1971.

Chapter 2. PEOPLE LIVE HERE

1. The titles of Kenneth Keniston's books indicate the thrust of each of his inquiries: *The Uncommitted: Alienated Youth in American Society* (Harcourt, Brace & World, Inc., 1965); *Young Radicals: Notes on Committed Youth* (Harcourt, Brace & World, Inc., 1968); *Youth and Dissent* (Harcourt Brace Jovanovich, 1971).

2. Erik H. Erikson, *Identity and the Life Cycle: Selected Papers*, Psychological Issues, Vol. I, No. 1 (International Universities Press, Inc., 1959). See especially pp. 88–94, "The Healthy Personality."

3. Theodore Roszak, *The Making of a Counter-Culture* (Doubleday & Company, Inc., 1969), p. xii.

4. *Ibid.*, p. xiii. Roszak interprets youth culture in terms of the "gurus" of the young—such as Norman O. Brown, Herbert Marcuse, Allen Ginsberg, Alan Watts, and Paul Goodman. He sees them expressing a need for visionary living and living in tune with nature.

5. Margaret Mead, *Coming of Age in Samoa* (William Morrow & Co., Inc., 1928).

6. Margaret Mead, *Culture and Commitment: A Study of the Generation Gap* (Natural History Press, 1970).

7. One should remember the viewpoint of Thomas S. Szasz,

The Myth of Mental Illness: Foundations of a Theory of Personal Conduct (Harper & Row, Publishers, Inc., 1961), that mental illness cannot be classified as disease, because it has no specific cause, treatment, or form of prevention.

8. Erikson, *op. cit.*, pp. 98 ff. For a theological understanding, see Lewis J. Sherrill, *The Struggle of the Soul* (The Macmillan Company, 1963).

9. The work of Elisabeth Kübler-Ross at the department of psychiatry, Billings Hospital, University of Chicago, has been a significant beginning. Her work with chaplains, students, and faculty at the University's Divinity School is becoming influential elsewhere. See her book *On Death and Dying* (The Macmillan Company, 1969).

10. The United Methodist Church has for some years designed a periodical and study guide specifically for older adults entitled *Mature Years,* Dewey D. Warren, editor (The Graded Press). This does not preclude participation with intergenerational groups but gives an opportunity for age-specific learning.

11. John F. Cuber and Peggy B. Harroff, *Sex and the Significant Americans: A Study of Sexual Behavior Among the Affluent* (Penguin Books, Ltd., 1966), is a study of the marriages of two hundred couples and indicates their own response to the dichotomy between principle and practice. Helen Colton, *What Adults Should Know About Sexuality* (Association Press, 1971), is an inquiry into contemporary life-styles.

12. Books on women's liberation proliferate. A good introductory statement of where women are with reference to the church may be found in the essays under the title *Women's Liberation and the Church,* ed. by Sally Doely (Association Press, 1971).

13. This is one of the concluding suggestions in John H. Westerhoff III, *Values for Tomorrow's Children* (Pilgrim Press, 1970), pp. 92 f.

Chapter 3. SCIENCE: TOWARD UTOPIA OR DOOM?

1. This is a thesis of Ian Barbour's *Issues in Science and Religion* (Prentice-Hall, Inc., 1966), pp. 44 f.

2. *Ibid.,* pp. 142–143.

3. James D. Watson, *The Double Helix: Being a Personal Account of the Discovery of the Structure of DNA* (Atheneum Publishers, 1968).

4. *Ibid.*, p. 174.

5. *Ibid.*, pp. 246 f.

6. *Ibid.*, p. 270.

7. Langdon Gilkey, *Religion and the Scientific Future: Reflections on Myth, Science, and Theology* (Harper & Row, Publishers, Inc., 1970), p. 32.

8. The extremes to which this attitude can be carried are protested by Michael Polanyi in *Personal Knowledge: Towards a Post-critical Philosophy* (The University of Chicago Press, 1958), in which he states the importance of experience as perceived by the person as a form of knowledge.

9. See the discussion of goals in Chapters 9 and 12.

10. Robert R. Boehlke, in *Theories of Learning in Christian Education* (The Westminster Press, 1962), sets forth the thesis that learning as perception, based on Gestalt psychology, is best able to convey the understanding of faith as response to the proclamation of the gospel.

11. This was the basic need structure outlined by Talcott Parsons, *Family Socialization and Interaction Process* (Free Press, 1955).

12. See Paul Ramsey, *The Patient as Person: Exploration in Medical Ethics* (Yale University Press, 1970), and Joseph Fletcher, *Morals and Medicine* (The Beacon Press, Inc., 1960).

13. See Paul Tillich, *Systematic Theology*, Vol. I (The University of Chicago Press, 1951), p. 238. On this point, John A. T. Robinson, in *Honest to God* (The Westminster Press, 1963), p. 22, quotes from Tillich's book of sermons, *The Shaking of the Foundations* (Charles Scribner's Sons, 1952), p. 57.

Chapter 4. SCIENCE APPLIED: THE USES OF TECHNOLOGY

1. "The Luddites Were Not All Wrong," by Wade Green and Soma Golden, based on an interview with Ezra Mishan, British economist, "apostle of antigrowth," with a discussion of his ideas (*The New York Times Magazine*, Nov. 12, 1971, p. 40).

2. Gilkey, *Religion and the Scientific Future*, p. 92.

3. *Ibid.*, pp. 92–94.

4. Norbert Wiener, *God and Golem, Inc.* (Massachusetts Institute of Technology, 1964). See also his *The Human Use of Human Beings: Cybernetics and Society* (Houghton Mifflin Company, 1950).

5. Andrew M. Greeley, *A Future to Hope In: Socio-religious Speculation* (Doubleday & Company, Inc., 1968), p. 123.

6. Among other books dealing with this area might be noted Jacques Ellul, *The Technological Society* (Alfred A. Knopf, Inc., 1964); Lewis Mumford, *The Myth of the Machine: The Pentagon of Power* (Harcourt Brace Jovanovich, 1970); Emmanuel G. Mesthene, *Technological Change: Its Impact on Man and Society* (Harvard University Press, 1970); and *The Evolving World and Theology*, ed. by Johannes Metz, *Concilium*, Vol. XXVI (The Paulist Press, 1967).

7. The periodical *The Living Light* has exploratory articles in this area—for example: "Periodic Religious Education: A Path Not Yet Explored," by Richard Reichert (Vol. VII, No. 1, Spring, 1970, pp. 57 ff.); "A Family Learning Center: A New Approach," by Michaela Ferren (Vol. VI, No. 3, Fall, 1969, pp. 62 ff.).

8. H. Marshall McLuhan, *The Gutenberg Galaxy: The Making of Typographic Man* (University of Toronto Press, 1962).

9. See H. Marshall McLuhan, *Understanding Media* (McGraw-Hill Book Co., Inc., 1964) and (with Quentin Fiore) *The Medium Is the Massage* (Bantam Books, Inc., 1970). For a critique of McLuhan and his reply, see *McLuhan: Hot and Cool*, ed. by Gerald Emanuel Stearn (The Dial Press, Inc., 1967).

10. Examples are *Media for Christian Formation: A Guide to Audio-Visual Resources*, ed. by William A. Dalglish, in two volumes (George A. Pflaum, Publisher, Inc., 1969, 1970); *Eye on the Arts*, a monthly bulletin of the St. Clement's Film Association, New York, N.Y.; and two volumes edited by Benjamin F. Jackson, Jr.: *Communication: Learning for Churchmen* (Abingdon Press, 1968) and *Television-Radio-Film for Churchmen* (Abingdon Press, 1969). The National Council of Churches' Office of Communication has a Department of Broadcasting and Film.

11. See Corita Kent's *Footnotes and Headlines: A Play-Pray Book* (Herder & Herder, Inc., 1967); also see Joseph Pintauro and Corita Kent, *To Believe in Things* (Harper & Row, Publishers, Inc., 1971).

12. The United Presbyterian Church U.S.A. developed and made available to radio and television stations such a series of spot announcements. Another series is available on film from Franciscan Communications Center of Los Angeles.

13. See Constantinos A. Doxiadis, *Ekistics: An Introduction to the Science of Human Settlements* (Oxford University Press, Inc., 1968). New towns, designed around the quality of living, are being developed in several countries, including England, Sweden, Finland, and the United States.

14. Lynn White, "The Historical Roots of Our Ecological Crisis," *Science,* March 10, 1967.

Chapter 5. SPEAKING ABOUT GOD

1. W. Norman Pittenger, "Bernard Meland, Process Thought and the Significance of Christ," *Religion in Life*, Vol. XXXVII, 1968, pp. 540–550; quoted in *Process Theology: Basic Writings*, ed. by Ewert H. Cousins (Paulist/Newman Press, 1971), pp. 210 ff. Pittenger has written a book on process theology, *Process and Christian Faith* (The Macmillan Company, 1968).

2. Dietrich Bonhoeffer, *Letters and Papers from Prison* (The Macmillan Company, 1953), especially pp. 162–165, 194–197, 208–210, 219.

3. John A. T. Robinson, *op. cit.*

4. William Hamilton and Thomas J. J. Altizer, *Radical Theology and the Death of God* (Bobbs-Merrill Company, Inc., 1966); Gabriel Vahanian, *The Death of God* (George Braziller, Inc., 1961); Paul van Buren, *The Secular Meaning of the Gospel: An Original Inquiry* (The Macmillan Company, 1963).

5. Richard L. Rubenstein, *After Auschwitz: Radical Theology and Contemporary Judaism* (Bobbs-Merrill Company, Inc., 1966).

6. Edward Schillebeeckx, *God and the Future of Man* (Sheed & Ward, Inc., 1968), p. 181.

7. Edward Schillebeeckx, *God and Man* (Sheed & Ward, Inc., 1969), p. 34. The book also contains a careful critique of John A. T. Robinson's *Honest to God,* with conclusions for the theological task today.

8. Edward Schillebeeckx, *Christ the Sacrament of the Encounter with God* (Sheed & Ward, Inc., 1963).

9. Leslie Dewart, *The Future of Belief: Theism in a World Come of Age* (Herder & Herder, Inc., 1966), pp. 186–206, *passim.*

10. Gregory Baum, *Man Becoming: God in Secular Experience* (Herder & Herder, Inc., 1966), Introduction, pp. vii–viii. See also Hans Urs von Balthasar, *The God Question and Modern Man* (The Seabury Press, 1967), a book concerned with the doctrine of man.

11. Martin E. Marty, *The Search for a Usable Future* (Harper & Row, Publishers, Inc., 1969), pp. 76–80, *passim.*

12. Martin E. Marty and Dean G. Peerman, eds., *New Theology,* annual volumes beginning in 1964 (The Macmillan Company).

13. Gordon R. Kaufman, *Systematic Theology: A Historical Perspective* (Charles Scribner's Sons, 1969).

14. Bernard J. Lonergan, *Insight: A Study of Human Understanding* (Philosophical Library, Inc., 1957). Also see *Collection: Papers by Bernard J. Lonergan,* ed. by F. E. Crowe (Herder & Herder, Inc., 1967). Significantly, the index gives references to Scripture, Aristotle, and Thomas Aquinas.

15. Ian T. Ramsey, *Religious Language: An Empirical Placing of Theological Phrases* (Alec R. Allenson, Inc., 1957). The originator of the discussion was Ludwig Wittgenstein, whose *Tractatus Logico-Philosophicus* (Harcourt, Brace & Company, 1922) is the fountainhead for the movement. Other scholars who have studied religious language include R. B. Braithwaite and Paul van Buren. One of the clearest interpretations of linguistic writers has been made by Randolph Crump Miller in *The Language Gap and God: Religious Language and Christian Education* (Pilgrim Press, 1970).

16. Karl Rahner, *Theological Investigations,* Vol. V (Helicon Press, Inc., 1966), Ch. 19, "What Is Heresy?" pp. 468 ff.

17. J. Deotis Roberts, *Liberation and Reconciliation: A*

Black Theology (The Westminster Press, 1971). Other books are James H. Cone, *A Black Theology of Liberation* (J. B. Lippincott, 1970), Albert B. Cleague, Jr., *Black Messiah* (Sheed & Ward, Inc., 1968), Major J. Jones, *Black Awareness: A Theology of Hope* (Abingdon Press, 1971), Joseph R. Washington, Jr., *The Politics of God: The Future of the Black Churches* (The Beacon Press, Inc., 1967).

18. Beginnings have been made by H. Herbert Richardson, *Toward an American Theology* (Harper & Row, Publishers, Inc., 1967); and Thomas F. O'Meara and Donald M. Weisser (eds.), *Projections: Shaping an American Theology for the Future* (Doubleday & Company, Inc., 1970).

19. Pierre Teilhard de Chardin, *The Divine Milieu: An Essay on the Interior Life* (Harper & Brothers, 1960).

20. Pierre Teilhard de Chardin, *The Phenomenon of Man,* rev. English ed. (Harper & Row, Publishers, Inc., 1965).

21. Alfred North Whitehead, *Process and Reality: An Essay in Cosmology* (The Macmillan Company, 1929).

22. Charles Hartshorne's earliest book was *Beyond Humanism: Essays in the New Philosophy of Nature* (Willett, Clark & Co., 1937). The University of Chicago Divinity School became a gathering place for theologians and philosophers holding this viewpoint, and some members of the "younger generation" are also products of the school. An excellent introduction to process theology is to be found in Cousins, *op. cit.* This anthology contains key selections from the writings of most process theologians and a fine bibliography of both their works and works about them.

23. Whitehead, *op. cit.,* p. 529.

24. John B. Cobb, Jr., *A Christian Natural Theology* (The Westminster Press, 1965).

25. Schubert M. Ogden, *Christ Without Myth: A Study Based on the Theology of Rudolf Bultmann* (Harper & Row, Publishers, Inc., 1961), and *The Reality of God and Other Essays* (Harper & Row, Publishers, Inc., 1966).

26. John B. Cobb, Jr., *God and the World* (The Westminster Press, 1969), pp. 67 f.

27. A discussion of the understanding of evil and judgment in the thought of Teilhard may be found in a volume by

Georges Crespy, *From Science to Theology: An Essay on Teilhard de Chardin* (Abingdon Press, 1968).

28. Daniel Day Williams has been constantly sensitive to "what present-day theologians are thinking" in his continuously revised volume on that subject, *What Present-Day Theologians Are Thinking,* 3d ed. rev. (Harper & Row, Publishers, Inc., 1967). His book *The Spirit and the Forms of Love* (Harper & Row, Publishers, Inc., 1968) brings this dimension into the discussion.

Chapter 6. WITNESS TO GOD

1. Hans W. Bartsch (ed.), *Kerygma and Myth: A Theological Debate,* by Rudolph Bultmann (and others) (Harper & Row, Publishers, Inc., 1961).

2. Ogden, *op. cit.*

3. James M. Robinson, *A New Quest of the Historical Jesus* (Alec R. Allenson, Inc., 1959). See also Reginald H. Fuller, *The New Testament in Current Study* (Charles Scribner's Sons, 1962).

4. Günther Bornkamm, *Jesus of Nazareth* (Harper & Row, Publishers, Inc., 1961).

5. A more conservative study made at this time was by Ethelbert Stauffer, *Jesus and His Story* (Alfred A. Knopf, Inc., 1960).

6. Wolfhart Pannenberg, *Jesus—God and Man* (The Westminster Press, 1968), p. 98.

7. *Ibid.*

8. Jürgen Moltmann, *The Theology of Hope* (Harper & Row, Publishers, Inc., 1967), p. 16.

9. *Ibid.*

10. Other books are Carl E. Braaten, *The Future of God: The Revolutionary Dynamic of Hope* (Harper & Row, Publishers, Inc., 1969); Dietrich Ritschl, *Memory and Hope: An Inquiry Concerning the Presence of Christ* (The Macmillan Company, 1968); Reubem A. Alves, *A Theology of Human Hope* (Corpus Books, 1969).

11. Jürgen Moltmann, *Religion, Revolution, and the Future* (Charles Scribner's Sons, 1969), p. 137.

12. Johannes B. Metz (ed.), *Faith and the World of Politics, Concilium*, Vol. XXXI (Paulist Press, 1968), p. 8.

13. *Ibid.*, p. 81.

14. Writings on religion and revolution: M. Richard Shaull, *Encounter with Revolution* (Association Press, 1955); Carl Oglesby and Richard Shaull, *Containment and Change* (The Macmillan Company, 1967); Martin E. Marty and Dean Peerman (eds.), *New Theology*, No. 5 (The Macmillan Company, 1970).

15. Pier Pasolini's movie *The Gospel According to St. Matthew* caught the possibility of a revolutionary interpretation to Jesus' teaching. Note, however, that the rock opera *Jesus Christ Superstar* portrays a highly personalized view of Jesus.

16. Langdon Gilkey, "Cosmology, Ontology and the Travail of Biblical Language," *Journal of Religion*, Vol. XLI (1961), pp. 794 f.

17. Brevard S. Childs, *Biblical Theology in Crisis* (The Westminster Press, 1970), p. 77.

18. *Ibid.*, p. 94.

19. Wolfhart Pannenberg (ed.), *Revelation as History* (The Macmillan Company, 1968). This essay was written in 1961, the year the Gilkey article was published.

20. James M. Robinson and John B. Cobb, Jr. (eds.), *The New Hermeneutic*, Vol. II of *New Frontiers in Theology* (Harper & Row, Pubishers, Inc., 1964). See also Gerhard Ebeling, *Word and Faith* (Fortress Press, 1963).

21. Note that the study materials published by Friendship Press for 1971–72 on the subject "Africa" are all written by blacks, and most are written by Africans. These materials are widely used by lay study groups.

22. See Gerhard E. Lenski, *The Religious Factor: A Sociological Study of Religion's Impact on Politics, Economics, and Family Life* (Doubleday & Company, Inc., 1961); Rodney Stark and Charles Y. Glock, *American Piety: The Nature of Religious Commitment* (University of California Press, 1968).

23. A study of these elements in the American heritage has been gathered by Sidney E. Ahlstrom in *Theology in America: The Major Protestant Voices from Puritanism to Neo-orthodoxy* (Bobbs-Merrill Company, Inc., 1967).

24. Florence M. Fitch, *One God: The Ways We Worship Him* (Lothrop, Lee & Shepard Co., 1944). Other books are: Leonard T. Wolcott and C. E. Muller, *Religions Around the World* (Abingdon Press, 1967); Sophia L. Fahs and Dorothy T. Spoerl, *Beginnings: Earth, Sky, Life, Death* (The Beacon Press, Inc., 1958).

Chapter 7. BEING THE CHURCH

1. "Dogmatic Constitution on the Church," *The Documents of Vatican II*, ed. by Walter M. Abbott (Guild Press, Inc., 1966), p. 17.

2. This formed an important aspect of my earlier book, *The Dynamics of Christian Education* (The Westminster Press, 1958). Cf. Ch. 2, "The Context of Christian Education," pp. 36 ff.

3. *Op. cit.*, p. 79.

4. Karl Rahner says: "Above all, a new theology must be found which is worthy of Vatican II and the task assigned to the church. It is not as though the theology of today were not good, but because it can become better" (*The Church After the Council* [Herder & Herder, Inc., 1966], p. 24). Other books in this area are Augustin Bea, *The Church and Mankind* (Franciscan Herald Press, 1967), and Avery R. Dulles, *The Dimensions of the Church: A Postconciliar Reflection* (The Newman Press, 1967).

5. Hans Küng, *Structures of the Church* (Thomas Nelson & Sons, 1964).

6. Hans Küng, *The Church* (Sheed & Ward, Inc., 1967).

7. Yves Congar, *Lay People in the Church: A Study for a Theology of the Laity* (The Newman Press, 1957). Congar has since written other books in this field. Hendrik Kraemer, *A Theology of the Laity* (The Westminster Press, 1959).

8. *Op. cit.*, pp. 281–291.

9. One such symposium is in the area of education: *Does the Church Know How to Teach? An Ecumenical Inquiry*, ed. by Kendig Brubaker Cully (The Macmillan Company, 1970). For lay discussion groups, see William B. Greenspun and William A. Norgren (eds.), *Living Room Dialogues* (Paulist

Press and National Council of Churches of Christ in the U.S.A., 1965), and William B. Greenspun and Cynthia C. Wedel (eds.), *Second Living Room Dialogues* (Paulist Press and National Council of the Churches of Christ in the U.S.A., 1967).

10. The Department of Educational Development of the National Council of Churches, Division of Christian Education, has a portfolio for the development of black curricular materials and resources, which is staffed by Olivia Pearl Stokes. See also *Spectrum,* July–August, 1971, an issue devoted to black religious education.

11. Kenneth Scott Latourette, *History of Christianity* (Harper & Brothers, 1953).

12. Ivan D. Illich, *Deschooling Society* (Harper Torchbook, Harper & Row, Publishers, Inc., 1971).

13. Paulo Freire, *op. cit.*

14. See books by Sally Cunneen, *Sex: Female; Religion: Catholic* (Holt, Rinehart and Winston, Inc., 1968); and Mary Daly, *The Church and the Second Sex* (Harper & Row, Publishers, Inc., 1968); and articles by Elizabeth Farians, who has worked on the Ecumenical Task Force on Women and Religion for the National Organization for Women.

Chapter 8. THE CHURCH AND ITS MISSION

1. The Department on Evangelism of the World Council of Churches, prior to the Fourth Assembly at Uppsala in 1968, issued a preparatory study in depth on the missionary structure of the congregation, which was entitled *The Church for Others* (Geneva, 1967).

2. A summary of such efforts has been made in the book by Rüdiger Reitz, *The Church in Experiment: Studies in New Congregational Structures and Functional Mission* (Abingdon Press, 1969).

3. This is a theme in my book *Christian Worship and Church Education* (The Westminster Press, 1967).

4. Schillebeeckx, *God and the Future of Man,* Ch. 3, "Secular Worship and Church Liturgy," p. 99.

5. Leslie Dewart, *op. cit.,* p. 206.

6. This is the point of view of F. Nile Harper. See his chapter "Prospects and Parables" in Kendig Brubaker Cully and F. Nile Harper (eds.), *Will the Church Lose the City?* (The World Publishing Company, 1969).

7. The name of Joseph Fletcher is connected with situation ethics. See his *Situation Ethics: The New Morality* (The Westminster Press, 1966). See also Paul L. Lehmann, *Ethics in a Christian Context* (Harper & Row, Publishers, Inc., 1963), James M. Gustafson and James T. Laney (eds.), *On Being Responsible: Issues in Personal Ethics* (Harper & Row, Publishers, Inc., 1968), Bernard Häring, *Morality Is for Persons* (Farrar, Straus and Giroux, Inc., 1970). Paul Ramsey has seemed to be more "law"-oriented. See his *Basic Christian Ethics* (Charles Scribner's Sons, 1950).

8. Very little work has been done on rethinking the meaning of Christian living. There was an issue of *Una Sancta* (Vol. XXI, No. 1, 1967) on the subject. John David Maguire's *The Dance of the Pilgrim: A Christian Style of Life for Today* (Association Press, 1967) is a brief introduction to a new style.

9. Harvey Cox, *The Feast of Fools: A Theological Essay on Festivity and Fantasy* (Harvard University Press, 1969); David L. Miller, *op. cit.;* Robert E. Neale, *In Praise of Play* (Harper & Row, Publishers, Inc., 1969).

10. Two books seeking new approaches are Jacques Ellul, *Prayer and Modern Man* (The Seabury Press, 1970) and Douglas Rhymes, *Prayer in the Secular City* (The Westminster Press, 1968).

Chapter 9. THE TEACHING-LEARNING PROCESS

1. Erik Erikson, *op. cit.*, pp. 55–88; Robert Havighurst, *Developmental Tasks and Education*, 2d ed. (Longmans, Green & Co., Inc., 1950).

2. For a newer book gathering together his thought, see Jean Piaget and Barbel Inhelder, *The Psychology of the Child* (Basic Books, Inc., 1969).

3. Ronald Goldman's study is contained in his book *Religious Thinking from Childhood to Adolescence* (Humanities Press, 1964). This is summarized and the methodological im-

plications are added in his *Readiness for Religion: A Basis for Developmental Religious Education* (The Seabury Press, 1968). The developmental view also has been explicated by David Elkind on the basis of his work with children. See his chapter, "The Development of Religious Understanding in Children and Adolescents," in *Research on Religious Development*, ed. by Merton P. Strommen (Hawthorn Books, Inc., 1971), pp. 655 ff.

4. Richard M. Jones, *Fantasy and Feeling in Education* (New York University Press, 1968).

5. Kathrene McLandress Tobey has written a book to help religion teachers use the senses: *Learning and Teaching Through the Senses* (The Westminster Press, 1970).

6. Basic work on creativity has been done by Jerome Kagan, who edited *Creativity and Learning* (The Beacon Press, Inc., 1967).

7. Burrhus Frederick Skinner, *Science and Human Behavior* (The Macmillan Company, 1953). See Ch. 23 on religion as a controlling agency, p. 350. See also his *The Technology of Teaching* (Appleton-Century-Crofts, Inc., 1968).

8. This goes back to the work of Kurt Koffka, *Principles of Gestalt Psychology* (Harcourt, Brace & Company, Inc., 1935). Much later it may be found in a book by Arthur W. Combs and Donald Snygg, *Individual Behavior: A Perceptual Approach to Behavior*, rev. ed. (Harper & Brothers, 1959). It is basic to the methodology of Carl R. Rogers, as seen in his *On Becoming a Person* (Houghton Mifflin Company, 1961) and *Freedom to Learn* (Charles E. Merrill Publishing Company, 1969).

9. Jerome Bruner, *Toward a Theory of Instruction* (Harvard University Press, 1966).

10. A helpful study with reference to the volunteer religion teacher has been made by Locke E. Bowman, Jr., as director of the Project for the Advancement of Church Education (PACE). See his *Education for Volunteer Teachers* (The Arizona Experiment, National Teacher Education Project, Scottsdale, Arizona, 1971). Two programs emanating from the project are Instroteach workshops and the Learning Laboratory.

11. Cooperative Curriculum Development, *Tools of Curriculum Development for the Church's Educational Ministry* (Warner Press, Inc., 1967).

12. These are outlined in the pamphlet *Christian Faith and Action: Designs for an Educational System* (Board of Christian Education, The United Presbyterian Church U.S.A.), and may also be found in the teacher's guide for each course of the *Christian Faith and Action* curriculum.

13. A useful guide for parish educational planning is *Educational Guide,* prepared for the educational plan of the Church of the Brethren (General Brotherhood Board, Elgin, Ill., 1968). This is introductory to what is called the *Keysort Library of Resources,* a carefully indexed card file with hundreds of entries.

14. Material on the use of the open classroom in England has been gathered by Joseph Featherstone, *Schools Where Children Learn* (Liveright Pub. Corp., 1971).

15. *Ibid.,* Part III.

16. Lawrence A. Cremin, *The Transformation of the School: Progressivism in American Education, 1876–1957* (Alfred A. Knopf, Inc., 1961).

17. The new interest in adult education in the Roman Catholic Church in the United States has been furthered by Gabriel Moran. See his *Design for Religion—Toward Ecumenical Education* (Herder & Herder, Inc., 1970).

Chapter 10. THE COMMUNITY AND LEARNING

1. Ivan Illich, *op. cit.*

2. Freire, *op. cit.,* p. 123.

3. A selection from their writings has been made by Beatrice and Ronald Gross in an anthology, *Radical School Reform* (Simon and Schuster, Inc., 1969). The book examines the protest, the new philosophies, and some examples of new practice.

4. A book that dreams of what education might be is *Education and Ecstasy,* by George B. Leonard (Delacorte Press, 1968).

5. This is the stance of Charles E. Silberman in *Crisis in*

the Classroom: The Remaking of American Education (Random House, Inc., 1970), the report of a study financed by the Carnegie Foundation. It should be noted that the radical reformers do not count him among their number.

6. James S. Coleman, *Adolescents and the Schools* (Basic Books, Inc., Publishers, 1965). For a pictorial documentary, see the film *High School*, 72 minutes, black and white, directed by Frederick Wiseman and distributed by OSTI, 264 Third Street, Cambridge, Mass. 02142.

7. See the account of her experiences in Sylvia Ashton-Warner, *Teacher* (Simon and Schuster, Inc., 1963).

8. The learning technique for the television series *Sesame Street* is essentially that of conditioning, with positive reinforcement: short blocks of material are repeated several times throughout the program, with a variety of methods and resources being employed to hold the attention of small children.

9. Andrew M. Greeley and Peter H. Rossi, *The Education of Catholic Americans* (Doubleday & Company, Inc., 1968).

10. *Religious Information and Moral Development: The Report of the Committee on Religious Education in the Public Schools of the Province of Ontario* (Toronto: Ontario Department of Education, 1969).

11. See my *The Dynamics of Christian Education*, Ch. 1.

12. This is outlined by Robert W. Lynn, *Protestant Strategies in Education* (Association Press, 1964), and the alternate place of the Sunday school is discussed in *The Big Little School: Two Hundred Years of the Sunday School* by Robert W. Lynn and Elliott Wright (Harper & Row, Publishers, Inc., 1971). The ambiguities in the pressure for religion in the schools are brought out in Robert Michaelsen's *Piety in the Public School* (The Macmillan Company, 1970).

13. See Michaelsen, *op. cit.;* also Theodore R. Sizer (ed.), *Religion and Public Education* (Houghton Mifflin Company, 1967), papers from a symposium on the subject held at Harvard University.

14. Among the few materials available at present is the *Through the Week* curriculum published by the Cooperative Publication Association for the National Council of Churches. This curriculum relates school studies to religious understand-

ings, in the areas of social studies, science, literature, and "the self."

Chapter 11. THE HOW OF TEACHING

1. Written resources on the method are few, but mention might be made of an article by Nathan Kollar, "Doing Christianity: The Action-Reflection Method," in *The Living Light*, Vol. VIII, No. 1, Spring, 1971. He also has an article "Action-Training Methodology and Theology" in *Theological Education*, Autumn, 1970, pp. 37 f. See also R. H. Bonthius, "Action Training, What Is It?" in *Theological Education*, Winter, 1970, p. 94. For a description of the method at work in a specific situation, see Kendig Brubaker Cully, "New Wine in an Old Bottle: Some Aspects of What Happens When Experimental Curriculum Is Undertaken in a Traditionalist Academic Environment," in *Shaping the Ministry for the 70's*, report of the 111th meeting of the Association of Seminary Professors in the Practical Fields, p. 57.

2. Huizinga, *op. cit.*

3. For books in this area, see Clark B. Abt, *Serious Games* (The Viking Press, Inc., 1970); Ray Glazier, *How to Design Educational Games* (Abt Associates, 1969); and Sarane S. Boocock and E. O. Schild (eds.), *Simulation Games in Learning* (Sage Publications, 1968). For the use of games specifically in religious education, see Martha Leypoldt, *Learning Is Change* (Judson Press, 1971).

4. See *Curriculum Improvement and Innovation: A Partnership of Students, School Teachers, and Research Scholars*, by William T. Martin and Dan C. Pinck (Robert Bentley, Inc., 1966).

Chapter 12. A FORECAST FOR THE CHURCH'S TEACHING MINISTRY

1. Deutsch, *op. cit.*, p. 8.
2. See Lyle E. Schaller, *The Local Church Looks to the Future* (Abingdon Press, 1971).

3. See Jean Piaget *et al.*, *The Moral Judgment of the Child* (Free Press, 1948).

4. See Thomas Green, *Work, Leisure, and the American Schools* (Random House, Inc., 1968), Robert Lee, *Religion and Leisure in America* (Abingdon Press, 1964).

5. Johannes Metz, *Theology of the World* (Herder & Herder, Inc., 1969), pp. 19–20.

6. James Michael Lee, *The Shape of Religious Instruction: A Social-Science Approach* (George A. Pflaum, Publisher, Inc., 1971). See the earlier discussion of goals in Chapter 9.

7. A thoughtful study of the future of religious education is included in Gustav K. Wiencke (ed.), *Christian Education in a Secular Society*, Yearbooks in Christian Education, No. 2 (Fortress Press, 1970).

DATE DUE
